MW01284041

Handbook of Practical Planning for
ARTISTS,
ART COLLECTORS,
and Their ADVISORS

SECOND EDITION

Ramsay H. Slugg

Defending Liberty
Pursuing Justice
AMERICAN BAR ASSOCIATION

SECTION OF REAL | TRUST &
PROPERTY | ESTATE LAW

Real Property, Trust and Estate Law 2019
Media/Books Products Committee

Carolyn P. Vinson, *Editor-in-Chief*
Candace M. Cunningham, *Editor-in-Chief Emeritus*
Phyllis M. Rubinstein, *Editor-in-Chief Emeritus*
Aen Walker Webster, *Editor-in-Chief Emeritus*

Real Property

Marcia Charney, *Managing Editor*
Ryan Almy, *Editor*
Joshua Crowfoot, *Editor*
Richard M. Frome, *Editor*
Jason Hirata, *Editor*
Thomas D. Kearns, *Editor*
Alan Keiser, *Editor*
Benjamin Lee, *Editor*

Trust and Estate

Elizabeth Lindsay-Ochoa, *Managing Editor*
Nathan Brown, *Editor*
Zisl Edelson, *Editor*
Amy Morris Hess, *Editor*
Marianne R. Kayan, *Editor*
Carly McKeeman, *Editor*
Sandra Sheets, *Editor*
Nancy E. Shurtz, *Editor*
Aen Walker Webster, *Editor*

Cover design by Jill Tedhams/ABA Design.
Interior design by Betsy Kulak/ABA Design.

The materials contained herein represent the opinions of the authors and/or the editors, and should not be construed to be the views or opinions of the law firms or companies with whom such persons are in partnership with, associated with, or employed by, nor of the American Bar Association or the Section of Real Property, Trust & Estate Law unless adopted pursuant to the bylaws of the Association.

Nothing contained in this book is to be considered as the rendering of legal advice for specific cases, and readers are responsible for obtaining such advice from their own legal counsel. This book is intended for educational and informational purposes only.

© 2019 American Bar Association. All rights reserved.

No part of this publication may be reproduced, stored in a retrieval system, or transmitted in any form or by any means, electronic, mechanical, photocopying, recording, or otherwise, without the prior written permission of the publisher. For permission contact the ABA Copyrights & Contracts Department, copyright@americanbar.org, or complete the online form at http://www.americanbar.org/utility/reprint.html.

Printed in the United States of America.

22 21 20 19 18   5 4 3 2 1

Library of Congress Cataloging-in-Publication Notice

Discounts are available for books ordered in bulk. Special consideration is given to state bars, CLE programs, and other bar-related organizations. Inquire at Book Publishing, ABA Publishing, American Bar Association, 321 N. Clark Street, Chicago, Illinois 60654-7598.

www.shopABA.org

Contents

About the Author

Ramsay H. Slugg is a frequent author and speaker on topics related to wealth-transfer planning, charitable planning, and planning with art and collectibles in particular. He is an active member of the Real Property, Trust and Estate Law Section of the American Bar Association, currently cochairs the Art and Collectibles Committee of its Income and Transfer Tax Planning Group, and is a past chair of its Charitable Planning and Organizations Group. Mr. Slugg is also a Fellow of the American College of Trust and Estate Counsel. He is also active in community affairs and is a past recipient of the President's Volunteer Service Award.

Mr. Slugg received his undergraduate degree from Wittenberg University (B.A., history, magna cum laude) and his Juris Doctorate from The Ohio State University. He practiced law in Ohio and Texas. He has previously served as an adjunct professor at both Texas Christian University and Texas Wesleyan (now A&M) University College of Law.

Mr. Slugg resides in Fort Worth, Texas, home to at least four great art museums, but spends as much time as possible in mid-coast Maine.

PART 1

Before We Get Started

Art is an asset of passion. This, coupled with its unique financial characteristics, makes it perhaps the most difficult asset to incorporate into an overall estate and financial plan. But this is imperative, and planning is always best done ahead of time, by the artist or the collector, rather than left to the family.

1

Introduction

Collecting art involves virtually every area of law, from property law, to contract law, to tax law, and so on. Property and contract law are probably the most essential, as they define the rights of all parties to the purchase and ownership of art.

This book, however, is not about "art law" per se. It is primarily about two related areas: first, planning for the ultimate disposition of art, including how to incorporate the wealth represented by the art into overall estate and financial planning, and second, practical considerations for collectors, while they are collecting and as they relate to the first area, planning for the ultimate disposition of the art. This second edition expands that discussion to commercially successful artists, who have unique planning issues.

As such, it is a book written for four people. Not just four individuals, mind you, but four types of people: first, the trusts and estates practitioner who has clients who collect or create art but who does not currently have substantial experience representing those clients who are art collectors or creators; second, art collectors who are in the process of determining the ultimate disposition of their collection; third, commercially successful artists who are in the same process (most of the discussion pertaining to artists is included in part 5); and fourth, allied professionals such as art advisors, risk-management advisors, and valuation advisors—in short, all of the professional advisors who should be working with the collector or artist as they prepare and implement their plan for the ultimate disposition of their art.

The book focuses on art. However, most of the discussion also applies to the broader world of collectibles: coins, stamps, antiques, collectible firearms, and the like. Several rules apply only to art, and those will be pointed out as they are discussed.

For those who are interested in a broader and deeper discussion of art law, selected additional resources—most notably, the seminal work, *Art Law* by Ralph E. Lerner and Judith Bresler, referenced throughout—are listed in the Resources section of this book.[1]

For many collectors, not only is their art among the most valuable assets that they own. They are also more passionate about their art than they are about their stocks, bonds, real estate, and maybe even the family business. They have spent considerable time, energy, and resources to develop their own expertise in art and have built a collection according to their personal aesthetic tastes and interests. Their interest may be in a particular artist, period, or medium, and they have likely developed relationships with artists, auction houses and galleries, and other collectors as well. Collecting art has gone way beyond a weekend hobby or a means to decorate their homes; it has become their passion.

Although they probably realize that there will be some sort of disposition of their art, they are most often more focused on the passion of collecting, not disposing. My experience has been that when they do consider the ultimate disposition of their collection, they are often overwhelmed by the seemingly endless number of choices of what to do. Their art is intensely personal to them and involves their passion and emotions much more than their pocketbook. When faced with all of these perceived choices, human nature takes over, and it all too often results in selecting the default planning option—doing nothing. It is not unlike a child at a toy store or candy store—their options seem endless, so they are hard-pressed to make a decision.

These same considerations apply to artists except that they are often dealing with a large inventory of their own works rather than a collection of others' works. This presents its own set of issues, which are addressed in part 5.

Often, the professional advisors to the collector or artist are not aware of the extent, or value, of their clients' collections, and planning consists of a simple, standard bequest of tangible personal property to the surviving spouse or, if not, then to the children or other heirs to divvy up as they agree. For a valuable collection, this simple solution will almost always lead to hard feelings and family conflict at the least—and perhaps to expensive, protracted litigation.

The value of art and other collectibles is significant, and it is estimated that between $4 and $6 trillion of collectibles will pass intergenerationally in the next 40 years.[2] Those collectibles, the most common of which is art, are owned by your clients, and they need your help in determining how to properly plan for the disposition of their collections.

The failure to plan for or face the disposition of these assets during the collector's lifetime may be costly on many fronts. Beyond federal income, estate, and gift tax considerations, the failure to plan may lead to a grossly inequitable division of estate assets or a fire sale from the estate. It will most certainly result in family discord—and perhaps litigation. Finally, the failure to plan will most assuredly lead to a disposition different from what the collector would have wanted if he or she had taken the time to properly plan.

This book is the result of working through the seemingly endless options with many collectors and artists, as well as observing the distress of families where planning has not occurred. That experience has helped me to develop a process to help collectors and artists focus on the few real planning options available for the disposition of their collections—specifically, their art. I will share examples of those experiences, as you, too, have likely encountered similar situations. The examples throughout the book will likely offer up some surprises as well and will help you, and your clients, to avoid those surprises.

"Art" is the subject of many books detailing the countless issues surrounding the ownership of art, proving that this subject cannot be covered in just one relatively short book, such as this. I, therefore, specifically exclude a number of art-related topics, which are simply beyond the scope of this book and, in some cases, the author's subject matter knowledge. I will not cover

- Art as an investment. I am not an expert on art, nor am I an expert on investments, so I am certainly not an expert on art as an investment. Although most collectors engage in this passion for aesthetic and personal reasons, a growing number of individuals are focusing more on the potential investment return from their art purchases, and the media are full of stories of the vast wealth represented by art. I will leave that topic to others much more qualified.

- Planning as it relates to art dealers. Special planning rules apply to art dealers. Although I mention some of those special rules in this book, reference additional resources at the end of the book, and may someday write another edition of this book that includes a discussion of considerations that pertain specifically to art dealers, this is not that book.

- Specific advice with respect to acquiring, displaying, storing, insuring, and transporting art. Each of these topics will be mentioned as it pertains to planning for the care and disposition of your collection, but specifics as to each of these topics are beyond the scope of this book. It does seem that I spend an increasing amount of time discussing these matters with collectors, so do not assume that just because your client has amassed a large collection they are engaged in appropriate collection management practices.

- Specific advice with respect to regulated or illegal assets, such as collectible firearms or art made from illegal-to-possess property, such as African ivory or Native American artifacts.

- Specific advice with respect to state law matters, including state income, estate, gift, and sales tax laws. Reference is made to these topics, and consideration should be given to these topics as part of the planning options discussed below because, where applicable, they could add significantly to the cost of any contemplated transaction. This is particularly true with respect to state sales tax, the collection of which has become an increased focus of state taxing authorities.

- Specific advice with respect to foreign or international laws or treaties. The world of art is truly international, and basic legal concepts and rights and duties may vary significantly from country to country. Extra care should be taken when a transaction is consummated in a foreign country.

- Sample documents. This is not a form book. I am licensed to practice law but do not currently engage in the practice of law, so I do not feel it is appropriate for me to provide samples of documents. For those who do seek sample forms to complete transactions or dispositive planning related to art, reference is made to *Art Law* by Lerner and Bresler. Of course, any such forms should always be used with care to ensure they comply with state law and are appropriate to the particular facts and circumstances of your transaction.

Planning as it relates to artists was specifically excluded from the first edition of this book. However, as more artists achieve commercial success, the financial aspects of their aesthetic achievements become more important. Furthermore, artists often leave significant amounts of inventory of their work behind, and inventory management and legacy management become particularly important. Special planning considerations and different tax rules apply to artists because their self-created works of art are in fact inventory, whereas the works of art held by collectors and investors are capital assets. For those reasons, I have added part 5 to this second edition to discuss these concerns.

Beyond that major addition, the focus of this book will continue to be to help collectors and those who work with collectors to plan for the ultimate disposition of their collections.

Some Definitions

Most books of a technical nature include a glossary of terms or definitions. Rather than including a glossary, I have chosen to list below a few definitions of terms you will encounter throughout the book. Additional, less frequently used terms are defined when first used in particular sections.

In alphabetical order, terms used throughout include the following:

AEA is the applicable exemption amount, which is the amount that may be transferred free of federal estate or gift tax. The AEA was increased by the Tax Cuts and Jobs Act ("2017 Tax Act"), signed into law effective January 1, 2018. The tax-free amount is $11,400,000 for 2019 and is indexed for inflation thereafter, until 2026, at which time the AEA is scheduled to revert to its 2017 level of $5,490,000, indexed for post-2017 inflation.

Art probably does not need a definition for anyone who is reading this book! Dictionaries define it broadly to include any creative or imaginative activity,[3] but for our purposes, let us think of it in a narrower context, perhaps as a creative or imaginative activity as expressed in paintings, sketches, lithographs, sculpture, and the like. Art is truly in the eye of the beholder.

Artist refers to an individual who creates art and, for our purposes, is engaged in the business of selling art to the public, be it directly or through a dealer.

Collector refers to someone who buys and sells art primarily for personal pleasure and is not a dealer or an investor. For federal income tax purposes, a collector usually cannot deduct expenses and losses incurred in collecting activities.[4]

Dealer refers to an individual who is engaged in the trade or business of selling art to customers—either directly or through a business entity. Whether one conducts a trade or business is primarily dependent on whether the person regularly engages in the activity, expects to make a profit from the activity, and holds themselves out to others as engaged in such activity.[5]

Donate refers to gratuitous transfers of art, during the collector's life, to museums or other charitable, nonprofit institutions. Also see " *Give* or *Gift.*"

Give or *Gift* refers to gratuitous transfers of art, during the collector's life, to family members or other individuals, other than charitable institutions.

Investor refers to someone who, individually or through an entity, buys and sells art primarily for investment rather than for personal use and enjoyment (a collector) or as a trade or business (a dealer). The primary difference between a collector and an investor is that the latter engages in the activity primarily to make a profit.[6]

IRC or *Code* refers to the Internal Revenue Code of 1986, as amended.

IRS or *Service* refers to the Internal Revenue Service.

Treas. Regs. refers to the regulations promulgated by the Department of the Treasury under the IRC.

Other resources, particularly *Art Law* by Lerner and Bresler, contain numerous case law citations further defining these terms.

Notes

1. RALPH E. LERNER & JUDITH BRESLER, ART LAW (Practising Law Inst., 4th ed. 2012).

2. Boston College's Social Welfare Institute estimates that of the $41 trillion that it projects will pass intergenerationally by 2052, between $4 and $6 trillion will represent art and antique assets.

3. *See, e.g.,* "art" as defined in the AMERICAN HERITAGE DICTIONARY (3d ed. 1994).

4. IRC § 183.

5. IRC § 162 and Treasury regulations thereunder. There are numerous cases addressing what constitutes a "trade or business," including, for example, Gajewski v. Commissioner, 723 F.2d 1062 (2d Cir. 1983), *cert. denied*, 459 U.S. 818 (1984).

6. IRC § 1221 and Treasury regulations thereunder.

2

The World of Art

Many books have been written about art, and the media are full of reports on a daily basis of record-setting art auction prices and stolen art. This book is not a substitute for all of that adventuresome reading! Collectors know all about the world of art; our focus here is on how to help them plan for the disposition of the art. Still, a bit of background helps to set the stage. According to industry reports, almost one-quarter of high-net-worth individuals consider "collectibles" as part of their "other investments." Among collectibles, art is the most frequently owned among the wealthy, with over one-quarter reporting that they own art. Art collectors have an average net worth between $15 and $25 million. And they are younger than in the past, with nearly one-quarter of collectors being 54 years old and younger.[1]

At the same time that collectors are wealthier and younger, the art markets continue to grow, with the worldwide public art auction market estimated at over $23 billion in 2017 and with the overall art market estimated to exceed $63 billion. This is led by the traditional art markets in the United States and the United Kingdom, but much growth has occurred in Asia, the Middle East, and Russia as well.[2]

Publicly sold art continues to grab the headlines. Art market headlines made much of the then anonymous buyer's purchase of one of the versions of Edvard Munch's *The Scream* at Sotheby's in May 2012 for $119.9 million, exceeding presale estimates by $40 million and setting what was then a record for the highest price paid for a public sale of art. That price has been exceeded more than 20 times since then.

Art prices continued to set records in 2017 with the following sales, to name a few:

- Roy Lichtenstein's *Masterpiece* sold for $165 million.
- Jean-Michel Basquiat's *Untitled* sold for $110.5 million.
- Vincent Van Gogh's *Laboureur dans un champ* sold for $81.3 million.
- Fernand Leger's *Constraste de formes* sold for $70.1 million.

And all of these sales were exceeded by the November 2017 public sale of Leonardo da Vinci's *Salvator Mundi* for $450.3 million, the highest public auction price to date (unless—or rather until—it is surpassed after this book is published). These five works of art sold for over $875 million! Add the next five pieces, and the total for the top 10 sales in 2017 exceeds $1 billion! And these are just a few, albeit more notable, examples of the high prices that are being paid for high-quality works of art.[3] Much of this has been driven by the contemporary art market, which has tripled in the last decade.

At the same time, art is not a "sure thing"; it has experienced volatility in value in the past and likely will in the future. A recent "charticle" in *Forbes* magazine suggests that art perhaps does not stack up as well as commonly thought compared to more traditional investments.[4] Accordingly, the author makes no representations or warranties about the suitability of art as an investment. In fact, one well-known art expert recently lamented the commercialization of art as an investment rather than appreciating art for its intrinsic and aesthetic worth.[5]

Still, even with all this talk of money and of art as an investment, most collectors report that they buy art for personal and aesthetic reasons, not financial reasons. In a report titled "Profit or Pleasure? Exploring the Motivations Behind Treasure Trends," only 10 percent of the 2,000 wealthy people from 17 countries who were interviewed reported that they bought art purely as an investment, whereas 75 percent cited enjoyment as a principal reason to buy art. Collectors are, by their very definition, more interested in the personal and aesthetic pleasure derived from collecting than in the financial benefits that may follow.[6]

And it may not just be the art itself. Attend Art Basel in Miami in December, or in its original home in June, and any number of major art fairs around the world, and you will encounter a party-like atmosphere, with art as the centerpiece but with the social connection important as well. Some suggest that buying art goes beyond a sense of social community; it engenders feelings of victory, cultural superiority, and social distinction. Buying expensive art is competitive as well and is often likened to trophy hunting.

Selling art, on the other hand, is often so difficult for collectors that they institutionalize the process and refer to "deaccessioning," much like a museum, rather than "selling." This leads to feelings of remorse and regret. Collectors like to hold on until the end, likening a sale to a death or divorce. Certainly, no one wants to be seen as "needing the money," as illustrated by the case in Dallas where a lawsuit was filed alleging breach of a confidentiality agreement over a prior sale of artwork by a seller wanting to raise cash discreetly.[7]

Against the backdrop of these most emotional of assets, we begin to examine the planning process for the inevitable, the ultimate disposition of the art.

The Planning Process

When I meet with collectors who have significant art collections, I often find that even if they have done comprehensive estate and financial planning with their traditional financial, real estate, and business assets, they are often at a loss as to what to do with their art collections. Even more often, I find that their confusion over what to do with their art has caused them to fail to complete their other planning.

The choices seem overwhelming. "I could give this piece to little Tommy. Or that piece to Suzie. And maybe this piece to the local food bank to sell at a charity auction. I'm not even sure if any of my family cares one bit for all of this beauty—it seems that they just want my money. Oh, I just don't know what to do!" As a result, they often do nothing.

And this default option of doing nothing means that the collection will end up with the personal representative of the estate, who often has little expertise in art and little if any direction as to an appropriate disposition.

It may end up being sold, often at undervalued prices, or it may be distributed to family members who may or may not share the collector's passion. So while this nonplanning approach is always an option, it will most likely end up being the most expensive in terms of administration—and the least desirable in terms of the ultimate disposition of the collection.

Well, that's our job—to help collectors know what to do and then to help them actually do it. It is ultimately their choice, but they need to know their options. And the options are not as numerous, or as overwhelming, as they may think.

Notes

1. 4 Spectrem, UHNW Investors (2011).

2. *Art Market Monitor*, http://www.artmarketmonitor.com.

3. Artprice, http://www.artprice.com; Sotheby's, http://www.sothebys.com; Christie's, http://www.christies.com.

4. Susan Adams, Jane Lee & Caleb Melby, *How Smart Is Art?*, Forbes 2014 Investment Guide Special Edition (2014).

5. *Why Buy Art?*, Economist, June 22, 2012.

6. Barclays, Profit or Pleasure? Exploring the Motivations Behind Treasure Trends (2012).

7. As reported in the Wall St. J., Dec. 5, 2013. Perhaps this is a good time to introduce the alerts that are provided by Aris Title, one of the few companies that provide title insurance for art. Sign up for alerts at Aris's website, http://www.aristitle.com. They are informative and often entertaining!

PART 2

The Ancillaries

There are at least four important matters—risk management, valuation, provenance and authenticity, and liquidity—that need to be addressed, regardless of the planning outcome. And as these issues are addressed, the most important piece of the collection—the inventory, or catalog—is a critical component of each. I usually raise these issues up front and make sure that the appropriate experts are brought into the planning process at the appropriate time.

3

Risk Management

Risk management is critical for sizable collections. For most, the decorative art and other collectibles we have around the house are likely adequately covered by our homeowner's insurance policy. But a really significant collection calls for a much more robust solution.

Risk management is first and foremost about putting into place safeguards to prevent damage to a collection. It is much better to prevent a claim for replacement or repair than it is to file a claim after the damage occurs.

Case Study

A collector owned an oil painting valued in the mid-eight figures. The collector was astute and experienced and had hired an expert to frame and hang the painting in his primary residence. The painting hung above a valuable antique console. Ancient Asian porcelain pieces were displayed on the console. And all of this was fronted by an antique Persian rug.

As is the case with many high-net-worth collectors, this collector had a second home. And while the collector was visiting the second home, an upstairs toilet in the primary residence started to leak. Water from the commode seeped along the floor, then gravity took hold, and the water ran down the inside of a wall . . . the wall where the valuable oil painting was hung! Although the water did not damage the painting

---

itself, the water gradually weakened the drywall. In time, the weight of the painting and its frame pulled the painting away from the wall, until it crashed down onto the console, shattering the porcelain and severely damaging the console and the rug.

Fortunately, the collector had appropriate property and casualty insurance in place with a carrier that was experienced in insuring fine art. The claim totaled in the tens of millions of dollars! Alternatively, a water leak detector and shutoff valve could have been in place for a total cost of a few hundred dollars.

Case in point—it is better, and much less expensive, both financially and emotionally, to prevent a claim than to file one!

Collectors should have a good grasp on the value of their collections and then engage an insurance specialist to determine the appropriate level and type of insurance. As mentioned above, this may be as simple as obtaining coverage under a homeowner's policy or requesting additional valuable items coverage that is separately scheduled from the homeowner's policy.

For collections of greater value, the collector (and advisory team) should engage an insurance professional who specializes in the high-net-worth space and who is able to provide not just an appropriate insurance policy but also risk-management practices concerning security and fire and smoke damage prevention. I like it when the advisor enters the home (or wherever the art is located) and, instead of looking at the art, is scanning the ceiling, walls, windows, doors, and flooring to determine if appropriate fire and theft systems are in place.

We often think that fire and theft are the most common causes of damage to art. However, accidental damage probably accounts for the highest volume of claims, followed by theft, fire, storm, or water damage, and my favorite category of all, "lost/mysterious disappearance"! The chances of actually experiencing a claim cannot always be controlled, but they can certainly be mitigated by working with a risk-management specialist.

Accidental damage is much more likely to happen if the art is moved from one residence to another or loaned to museums. In those cases, experts should again be used to properly pack, handle, and transport valuable works of art.

In addition to risk avoidance/mitigation, policy coverage is important. Some policies exclude coverage for damage caused by faulty packing, and others may exclude coverage for damage caused by flood or mysterious disappearance (I just love that term!).

If you loan your art to museums, make sure that insurance coverage is in place at all times: from the time it is packed at your location, through transportation, to installation and display . . . and then all over again when the art comes home. Museums are aware of the importance of this and can work with you and your insurance specialist to address any concerns.

Again, the key here is taking steps to avoid a claim. That is much more important than focusing on the claims process itself. And this is usually much broader than imagined and covers proper framing and hanging, or other installation, of artwork; water leak detection; periodic inspection of the collection to detect flaws (especially with respect to installation); and, of course, the more obvious fire, smoke, and theft prevention. A restoration specialist with whom I have worked advises that nothing lasts forever and everything needs a tune-up.

Risk management does not end at home. If any of the art is to be transported to another location or placed into storage, either during life or during estate administration, competent experts should be engaged to properly pack, transport, and store the art.

Who Stole My Art?

Most art thieves do not look like Pierce Brosnan in the remake of *The Thomas Crown Affair*. In fact, most art thieves are closer to home, and the first suspects when art is stolen are relatives, particularly relatives with substance abuse problems.

Art theft is big business, and most art that is stolen is never recovered. According to the Federal Bureau of Investigation (FBI), only about 5 percent of stolen art is recovered. So the best course of action, as with all risk management, is to try to prevent the theft in the first place. This begins at home, with an appropriate security system, but also with safeguards and background checks on household employees and contractors who have access to the art. Security should also extend to any off-site storage facility.

Provenance considerations, discussed in chapter 5, come into play here as well. If stolen art is recovered, then proof of ownership will be required to reclaim the art.

Inventories

From a planning point of view, an invaluable side benefit of appropriate risk management is an inventory. A collector, without even knowing it, has an inventory of sorts if he or she has maintained bills of sale and catalogs of sales where art was purchased. Beyond this, the company writing insurance to cover the collection will require an inventory, and may even assist the collector in building a form of inventory if they do not already have one.

As a planner, the inventory becomes a crucial document, helping the collector to express the "four Ws"—What goes Where, to Whom, and When. It will also provide a road map to the eventual estate fiduciary and the preparer of Form 706, Federal Estate Tax Return. In fact, I tell collectors that their inventory may well be the most important part of their collection!

Case Study

A collector had a massive collection—not so much in terms of dollar value as in terms of number of pieces. The collector hired a professional videographer, who walked through the house filming as the collector described each piece or part of the collection—what it was, where he obtained it, an approximate price and value, and where he thought the piece should eventually go, be it to a particular family member, to a particular museum or other charity, or to an estate sale to be sold. Copies of the video (now on disc) are with the insurance company, the lawyer, and the trust department that will serve as his executor.

That oral inventory has also been reduced to writing, in the form of a spreadsheet. This helps greatly in the planning process. It is, of course, up to the lawyer to make sure those wishes are properly documented and incorporated into the overall wealth-transfer plan.

Finally, making the video was fun. The client is a bit of an actor, and he was able to recount his life story with great flair and drama.

An inventory can take many forms, and the value and scope of the collection will dictate what is appropriate in any given situation. It should, at a minimum, include a description of each piece (including name, if any), artist name, acquisition date, where and from whom it was purchased, purchase price, condition (including any known repairs), and its physical location. Depending on the significance of the piece, the collector may want to make note of any exhibits or tours in which the piece has been included. This inventory can be expanded as appropriate, including a listing of any research materials that reference the piece and any externally maintained registries that include this and other pieces by the artist.

As the collection grows, so should this inventory. The collector may wish to photograph each piece and assign it an identification number, which allows for better organization of the inventory. The inventory may also include measurements, medium, and so on. All of this helps to identify and authenticate each piece, as well as assist in the risk-management process discussed above. Finally, this history greatly assists if a theft takes place or any questions of provenance arise.[1]

For those who do not have the time or inclination to physically prepare their own inventory, there are companies that provide this service. Again, the scope of work will be dependent on the size and value of the collection; options range from "do it yourself" smartphone applications, where you take a picture of the item and then type in relevant information, to a more concierge-like service, where one or more representatives photograph each piece and record all relevant information.

Whatever the form and extent of inventory used, it should be periodically updated to reflect changes in the collection.

Case Study

A collector had a modest collection, in terms of both value and number of pieces, but many pieces had great sentimental value and had been in her family for over 100 years. She was recently widowed and wanted to make sure that her children and grandchildren knew the history of each piece, all of which were located in the home where her children were raised.

She created a spreadsheet that listed each item by category (paintings, oriental rugs, furniture, etc.). For each item, the spreadsheet listed the particular piece, its physical location, how and when it was acquired (purchase or inheritance), cost (if she purchased the item), approximate value, and any history that she cared to pass on about the piece.

Certain items were separately scheduled for insurance purposes, but the main reason for the inventory was to help pass on her family's legacy as represented by collectibles held dear to them.

Note

1. For more information regarding inventories, you may wish to read MICHAEL MENDELSOHN, *Protecting Your Collection—Inventory, Preservation, and Insurance, in* LIFE IS SHORT, ART IS LONG chap. 7 (Acanthus, 2d ed. 2006–2007). For more on stolen art, *see* MICHAEL MENDELSOHN, *Provenance, in* LIFE IS SHORT, ART IS LONG, *supra,* chap. 5; and Daniel Grant, *Best Ways to Protect Your Art: Security Experts Offer Tips on Safeguarding Art Collections,* WALL ST. J., Nov. 10, 2013, p. 15. *See also* JAMES L. HALPERIN ET AL., *Safeguarding Your Collection, in* THE COLLECTOR'S HANDBOOK chap. 3 (Ivy Press, 10th ed. 2016).

4

Valuation

Valuation is critical to the entire planning process, whether the plan involves selling art, giving art to family members, or donating art to charity, and whether those sales or transfers take place during life or at death. Appraisals are required for any taxable transfers, and must be filed with Form 709, Federal Gift Tax Return, and Form 706, Federal Estate Tax Return. Appraisals are also required for charitable transfers where the value of the donation is above $5,000, as is appropriate substantiation. Finally, appraisals will be required to support any loans against the collection and will likely be required by insurers. Beyond all of these requirements, a periodic appraisal or valuation review of the collection should be considered a "best practice" for collectors.

Fair Market Value

The general rule for federal income, estate, and gift taxes is that transferred property is to be valued at its fair market value. Fair market value is itself defined generally in the Treasury regulations promulgated under the Internal Revenue Code (IRC) as the price at which property would change hands between a willing buyer and a willing seller, neither being under any compulsion to buy or to sell and both having reasonable knowledge of the relevant facts.[1] Relevant factors to be taken into consideration in determining fair market value include the cost or sales price of the property, sales prices of comparable items, and expert opinions.

In most cases, the cost of the property in the seller's or transferor's hands provides the best evidence of value, if the transfer of the property occurs shortly after it was purchased by the transferor. The Tax Court and other courts have followed this principle in a number of cases. For example, in *Hunter v. Commissioner*, a Tax Court memorandum decision, the taxpayer purchased a collection of prints for approximately one-fourth to one-third of the price at which they would be listed for retail sale and then donated the prints to charity. The taxpayer's claimed federal income tax charitable deduction at the supposed fair market value was reduced to the taxpayer's cost rather than the list price. The same principle has been followed in numerous other valuation cases.[2] Most of these cases involved charitable contribution schemes with no real economic substance, whereby the taxpayer would purchase an item for well under its purported value, hold the item beyond the long-term capital gain holding period, and then donate the item for its supposedly higher value. Gems, lithographs, books, art, and other collectibles have all been used in these tax shelter schemes.[3]

On the other side of the transaction, if the property is sold by the transferee shortly after the transfer, the sales price may once again be the best evidence of value. One such example of this is found in Revenue Procedure 65-19, which advises that the sale of a collection at public auction or via classified advertisement within a reasonable period of time after the collector's death will generally set the value of the collection for estate tax purposes.[4]

More often than not, there will not be either a purchase or a sale in close proximity in time to when the collector makes a transfer requiring a valuation. Furthermore, the guidance provided in the Treasury regulations assumes the existence of a retail market for the particular item being valued, which most often does not apply to unique pieces of art. Therefore, most of the time, a collector making a gift to family members or a donation to charity, or a personal estate representative acting on behalf of a deceased collector, will need to obtain an appraisal.

Appraisals and Appraisers

Revenue Procedure 66-49 set forth the original guidelines for an appraisal to support the federal income tax charitable deduction for contributions of tangible personal property, including art.[5] Notice that the information that should be included in the appraisal closely dovetails with the information that should be included in an inventory, as outlined in chapter 3.

The revenue procedure stated that an appraisal should include the following:

1. A complete description of the object, including the size, subject matter, medium, name or names of artists, approximate date of creation, and interest transferred.
2. The cost, date, and manner of acquisition.
3. A history of the item, including proof of its authenticity.
4. A photograph of a size and quality sufficient to identify the subject matter fully, preferably a 10-inch by 12-inch or larger print.
5. A statement of the factors on which the appraisal was based, including the following:
   a. The facts about the sales of other works by the same artist or artists, particularly on or around the valuation date;
   b. Quoted prices in dealers' catalogs of the works by the artist or artists or of other comparable artists;
   c. The economic state of the art market at or around the time of valuation, particularly with respect to the particular property being valued;
   d. A record of any exhibitions at which the particular art object was displayed; and
   e. A statement as to the standing of the artist in the profession and in the particular school, time, or period.

These requirements have been modified somewhat over time, most notably by the Tax Reform Act of 1984[6] and the Pension Protection Act of 2006.[7] Most significant are (1) the addition of substantiation requirements, including the requirement that an appraisal support any federal income tax charitable deduction for a contribution of tangible personal property, including art, the claimed value for which exceeds $5,000, and (2) further definition of the terms "qualified appraisal" and "qualified appraiser."

For a federal income tax charitable deduction, the threshold amount requiring an appraisal is $5,000. That amount applies to any single item or to an aggregate of similar items donated during the same calendar year. Once reached, the taxpayer must

1. Obtain a qualified appraisal for the contributed property.
2. Attach a fully completed appraisal summary to the federal income tax return on which the taxpayer first claims the deduction for the contribution.
3. Maintain certain records about the contribution.

This is in addition to the general substantiation requirement of obtaining a contemporaneous written acknowledgment of the contribution, stating that no goods or services were received. The failure to provide this information will result in the denial of the federal income tax charitable deduction.[8]

The Tax Reform Act of 1984 further defined the term "qualified appraisal." A "qualified appraisal" means an appraisal prepared by a qualified appraiser no more than 60 days before the date of contribution. The appraisal must be signed and dated by a qualified appraiser who states that the appraisal fee is not based on a percentage of the value of the appraised property. The appraisal must include

1. A detailed description of the property;
2. The physical condition of the property;
3. The date or expected date of contribution;
4. The terms of any agreement or understanding entered into or expected to be entered into by or on behalf of the donor that relates to the use, sale, or other disposition of the property contributed;
5. The name, address, and taxpayer identification number of the appraiser;

6. A detailed description of the appraiser's background and qualifications;
7. A statement that the appraisal was prepared for income tax purposes;
8. The date on which the property was valued;
9. The appraised fair market value of the property;
10. The method of valuation used to determine the fair market value;
11. The specific basis for the valuation, such as comparable sales transactions; and
12. A description of the fee arrangement between the donor and the appraiser.

In addition, the appraisal must be received by the donor before actually filing the income tax return.[9]

The Pension Protection Act of 2006 added to the appraisal requirement, requiring the appraiser to acknowledge the understanding that a substantial or gross valuation misstatement resulting from the appraisal could subject the appraiser to civil penalties under certain circumstances.[10] This is in addition to the previous requirement that the appraiser acknowledge that the intentionally false or fraudulent overstatement of value in the appraisal could lead to civil penalties and aiding and abetting penalties.

It is clear that more and more emphasis is being placed on the qualifications of the appraiser and on the relationship between the appraiser and the taxpayer. According to the Pension Protection Act, a "qualified appraiser" is one who

1. Has earned an appraisal designation from a recognized professional appraisal organization or has otherwise met minimum education and experience requirements set forth in regulations;
2. Regularly performs appraisals for pay; and
3. Meets other requirements that the Internal Revenue Service (IRS) may prescribe in regulations or other guidance.

Further, such an individual must demonstrate verifiable education and experience in valuing the property type being appraised and must not have been prohibited from practicing before the IRS at any time over the three-year period ending on the appraisal date.[11]

These heightened requirements make it imperative that the collector, or collector's representatives, examine the appraiser's qualifications. And just because someone is an expert in one area does not mean that he or she is an expert in all areas. Therefore, care must be exercised when selecting an appraiser, and examination should be made of his or her expertise and experience with the particular type of art to be appraised.

Further guidance is provided in IRS Publication 561, *Determining the Value of Donated Property*. Though directed specifically toward donations to charity of tangible personal property, it sets forth useful considerations in determining fair market value; discusses valuations of paintings, antiques, and other objects of art specifically; and sets forth the appraisal rules for donations of this type of property to charity.[12]

What to File

If the collector wishes to gift art during life and the amount of the gift is in excess of the annual exclusion amount (currently $15,000), a qualified appraisal must be filed with Form 709, Federal Gift Tax Return.[13]

If the collector wishes to donate the art to charity during life, a qualified appraisal will be required if the value of the transferred property is more than $5,000. The appraisal report must include a complete description of the object, indicating the size, subject matter, medium, name of the artist, and approximate date created, as well as the other information set forth above. This appraisal requirement is also part of the substantiation requirements.[14] Form 8283, Noncash Charitable Contributions, including the appraisal summary in section B of the form, must be attached to Form 1040, Federal Income Tax Return, to claim a charitable deduction. If the donation is more than $500,000, then the appraisal itself must be attached to the Form 1040. Failure to comply with the substantiation requirements, as discussed above and in chapter 9, may result in the entire federal income tax charitable deduction being denied.

If the appraisal is part of the estate administration process, then an appraisal will be required if the decedent owned any one piece worth more than $3,000 or a collection of similar items worth more than $10,000. An appraisal of the items must be attached to Form 706, Federal Estate Tax Return. The appraisal must be prepared by an expert under oath and must include a statement setting forth the appraiser's qualifications.[15]

Those appraisals are required for federal income, estate, and gift tax purposes. Beyond that, lenders will require an appraisal of the collection that is serving as collateral, and it is likely that any insurer will require an appraisal of what is covered by the insurance policy. It is also likely that lenders and insurers will require annual updates, though perhaps not full-blown appraisals each year. Finally, whether required or not, a periodic appraisal of the collection should be considered a best practice. How often a collector should update valuations depends on the type of art involved, as the values of different types of art fluctuate differently. For example, values of Masters are generally more stable than those of contemporary art.

For more significant pieces and collections, it may be advisable to obtain more than one appraisal. It is not uncommon for different appraisals to result in significantly disparate valuations.

Case Study

A collector was contemplating a wealth-transfer strategy in which 12 pieces of art would be transferred by gift via a family limited partnership and several trusts. An appraisal would be required to support the valuation of the art, as well as the value of the partnership interests being transferred.

The collector decided to obtain two appraisals. The total value of the 12 pieces was approximately the same in both appraisals. However, the individual value of the two more significant pieces were reversed in the two appraisals, with one valuing the two pieces at $7 million and $4 million and the other valuing the same pieces at $4 million and $7 million.

Both appraisals were completed by qualified appraisers, noted in the field of appraising art. This case shows that appraisals are a bit of an inexact science and that reasonable, competent appraisers may differ in opinion.

It was perhaps this uncertainty in the valuation process that caused Congress to create the IRS Art Advisory Panel in 1968. The Panel, which consists of approximately 25 art experts, including auction house representatives, dealers, and curators, assists the IRS's Art Appraisal Services when reviewing artwork or items with an appraised value of $50,000 or more. The Panel meets several times each year to review appraisals submitted to them. The Panel is not told whether the appraisals are submitted to substantiate an income tax charitable deduction or an estate or gift tax charitable deduction. The Panel's decision as to value in a particular case, although advisory, has in fact become the official position of the IRS on valuation of the item or collection in question.

During 2016, the most recent year for which a report is available at time of publication, the Panel reviewed 555 items, with a total value of $503,135,185, representing 63 different taxpayer cases. The Panel recommended no change to the value of 222 items (40 percent of the total number of items submitted), recommended increases to 202 items (37 percent of the total number of items submitted), and recommended decreases to 131 items (23 percent of the total number of items submitted). The average increase to items that were adjusted upward was $906,550. These percentages are generally in line with previous years and perhaps give a collector an idea of what to expect if they are subject to audit and the Panel is asked to provide advice to the IRS's Art Appraisal Services.[16]

It is also possible for a collector to obtain an advance ruling from the IRS, assisted by the Art Advisory Panel, as to valuation. The IRS states that this is for income tax purposes only. This procedure is detailed in Revenue Procedure 96-15.[17] Requirements include the following:

- The ruling request must be made after the property is transferred to the qualifying charity;
- The taxpayer must have obtained a qualified appraisal;
- At least one of the items transferred must have a value of at least $50,000; and
- A copy of Form 8283 and the appraisal must be attached to the ruling request.

The fee to obtain the ruling is $6,500 for the first three items, plus $300 for each additional item. The ruling, once issued, is binding on the IRS. The taxpayer may dispute the ruling by attaching it to the tax return that reports the transfer along with any additional information in support of the disputed value.

There is not a hard-and-fast rule as to whether it is advisable to seek such a ruling. Some advisors are in favor of seeking a ruling; others are not. And much depends on the particular set of facts. Those who seek a ruling as to valuation are advised to use an attorney or accountant who has experience in this area. The ruling request itself should include a qualified appraisal, prepared by an expert in the particular art area, that includes detailed descriptions of the pieces being appraised, an analysis of comparable works that have been sold within a reasonable time of the valuation date, and substantiation of the piece's authenticity.

Although the IRS takes the position that an advance ruling will be issued only for income tax purposes, the revenue procedure is in fact applicable to gift and estate tax returns as well, as long as all of the requirements of the revenue procedure are met.

Case Study

Although the Art Advisory Panel is made up of top experts in the field, even they are not infallible. Consider the case of *Canyon*, Robert Rauschenberg's famous collage, which was part of the estate of Ileana Sonnabend, who passed away in 2007 at the age of 92. The estate of Sonnabend, a well-known art collector and dealer, was valued at $876 million, and her estate paid $331 million in federal estate tax and $140 million in New York State estate tax.

The estate included *Canyon*, valued at zero by the estate, as supported by several qualified appraisals. The appraisals placed this value on *Canyon* because it included a stuffed bald eagle, which cannot be legally sold. Sonnabend had obtained a special permit to retain *Canyon* when the federal prohibition was passed.

The IRS, backed by the Art Advisory Panel, disagreed and valued *Canyon* at $65 million. The IRS sent the estate a notice of deficiency for $29 million in additional estate tax, plus a "gross valuation misstatement" penalty (discussed below) of $11.7 million. The IRS view was that even though *Canyon* could not be sold legally, a market exists for stolen and illegal goods. The Art Advisory Panel did not even take the possibility of an illegal sale into account and instead viewed the piece solely for its artistic value, without regard to any restrictions on sale.

The IRS position is actually in accord with its long-held practice of finding that contraband items (such as illegal drugs, stolen art, stolen jewels, and protected antiquities properly belonging to Native Americans or foreign governments) still have value. Indeed, the illegal market for artwork that is stolen or of questionable provenance is said to be the third-largest illegal market in the world, behind drugs and guns. Those cases are mostly different from *Canyon*, where there was no intent to deal in contraband. Nonetheless, the IRS maintained its position, settlement talks stalled, and the matter ended up in tax court.

The case was eventually settled, reportedly for $0! *Canyon* will remain roosted at the Metropolitan Museum of Art in New York City.[18]

Valuation Penalties

Valuations are important—not just because they can help you plan but also because incorrect valuations can cost money in the form of tax penalties.

For federal income tax purposes, IRC § 6662(e) imposes an accuracy-related penalty for any "substantial valuation misstatement." If the claimed valuation is 200 percent or more of the correct amount, the penalty imposed is 20 percent of the tax underpayment. If the claimed valuation is 400 percent or more of the correct amount, the penalty increases to 40 percent of the underpaid tax.

For example, if the taxpayer claimed an income tax charitable deduction of $20,000, but the painting was really worth only $8,000 (as finally determined on audit), with the result that the tax due was increased by $4,000, then the penalty would be 20 percent of that amount, or $800.

For federal estate and gift tax purposes, IRC § 6662(g) imposes a 20 percent penalty if the value shown on the return is 65 percent or less of the value ultimately determined. The penalty increases to 40 percent if the value shown on the return is 40 percent or less of the value ultimately determined.

For example, a painting was listed as being worth $25,000 on the federal estate tax return. However, it was ultimately determined that the painting is worth $100,000. This would give rise to a penalty equal to 40 percent of the federal estate tax attributable to the difference. Assuming an estate tax rate of 40 percent, the penalty would be $12,000 ($75,000 difference × 40 percent tax rate × 40 percent penalty).

The good news—if there is any—is that the IRS may waive these penalties if the taxpayer is able to establish that there was a reasonable basis for the valuation used and the claimed deduction was made in good faith.[19]

Best Practice

In addition to an appraisal being required by federal tax law to support valuation for income, estate, and gift tax purposes, it is likely that anyone providing insurance coverage will require an initial appraisal and periodic updates. Lenders who make art loans to collectors will also require an initial appraisal and periodic updates.

But even in situations where collectors are not currently required by law to have an appraisal (that is, no gifts or donations are currently being made) or required by service providers to have an appraisal (there are no loans or no insurance), collectors should still consider having an appraisal of their collection, with periodic updates. The appraisal and the inventory that will likely be a part of the appraisal are invaluable in assisting the collector with making decisions about the collection and about whether to transfer the art by gift to individuals or by donation to charities, whether to borrow against the art, and whether to insure the art if they have not already done so. And appraisals should be kept current, to reflect current market valuations. This information will also be invaluable to the personal representative of the collector's estate.

appraisal and inventory would help you to know what to loan pieces-

Recent Cases

Since the publication of the first edition of this book, two interesting valuation cases have been filed in the U.S. Tax Court. One case has been litigated and reported, but the other case has not been decided as of the time of publication of this edition.

In *Estate of Kollsman v. Commissioner*,[20] the U.S. Tax Court held that an art collector's estate significantly underreported the value of two artworks for estate tax purposes. The estate relied on purported appraisals by an auction house specialist who the court felt had an incentive to understate the values shown in the appraisals in order to win the right to later auction the works. In addition, the court found that the values reported by the estate were unpersuasive because the specialist exaggerated the dirtiness of the paintings and failed to adjust his appraisals after one of the works sold at auction for approximately five times more than the reported value. Conversely, the court found the IRS expert's valuations to be acceptable, although it allowed a 5 percent discount for the risks associated with cleaning both paintings, a 10 percent discount to the value of one painting by reason of its condition, and an additional 10 percent discount to the value of the other painting because of issues surrounding its attribution. Thus, the court found the values of the paintings to be nearly four times the amounts reported by the estate. This case shows the importance of using independent, qualified appraisers who provide appraisals in accordance with the rules set forth above.

In 2017, the estate of Lisa de Kooning filed a petition in the U.S. Tax Court after the IRS increased the value of the estate by $231 million, resulting in a $92 million tax bill.[21] The estate included a large collection of artwork, including 57 paintings, 83 sculptures, and 51 drawings by her father, Willem de Kooning, the famous Dutch-American abstract expressionist. Originally, the estate had appraised the collection at $231.4 million but discounted the value of the collection by nearly 60 percent for the paintings and 85 percent for most of the sculptures. The estate claimed these discounts to accommodate the "block" of artwork that could be introduced into the market. By increasing the estate's tax liability, the IRS determined that the estate could not apply "blockage discounts" to the value of the artwork.

Although it is possible that a collector could own a sufficient amount of a particular artist's works that a blockage discount could apply, both for planning purposes and for estate valuation purposes, it is more likely that a blockage discount would apply to an artist's estate. Therefore, a fuller discussion of blockage discounts is included in chapter 18.

Notes

1. IRC §§ 170, 2031, 2512; TREAS. REG. §§ 20.2031-6, 25.2512-1, 1.170A-1(c)(2).

2. Hunter v. Comm'r, 51 T.C.M. (CCH) 1533 (1986). *See also* Anselmo v. Comm'r, 80 T.C. 872 (1983), *aff'd*, 757 F.2d 1208 (11th Cir. 1985); Ford v. Comm'r, 46 T.C.M. (CCH) 1353 (1983).

3. *See* RALPH E. LERNER & JUDITH BRESLER, ART LAW 1244 (Practising Law Inst., 4th ed. 2012).

4. Rev. Proc. 65-19, 1965-2 C.B. 1002.

5. Rev. Proc. 66-49, 1966-2 C.B. 1257.

6. Tax Reform Act of 1984, § 155(a) and Treasury regulations thereunder.

7. Pension Protection Act of 2006.

8. Treas. Reg. § 1.170A-13(c).

9. Treas. Reg. § 1.170A-13(c)(3)(iv)(B).

10. Notice 2006-96, § 3.04(2), 2006-46 I.R.B. 902.

11. IRC § 170(f)(11)(E)(ii), (iii).

12. I.R.S. PUB. NO. 561, DETERMINING THE VALUE OF DONATED PROPERTY (rev. Apr. 2007), most readily obtained by visiting http://www.irs.gov.

13. See Instructions to Form 709, Federal Gift Tax Return, most readily obtained by visiting http://www.irs.gov. According to Treasury Regulation § 301.6501(c)-1(f)(2), in order for a gift tax return to begin the running of the statute of limitations, the gift must be adequately disclosed. A gift will be considered adequately disclosed if the return includes (1) a full and complete Form 709; (2) a description of the transferred property and any consideration received by the donor; (3) the identity of and relationship between the donor and donee; (4) if the property was transferred to a trust, the trust's EIN and a brief description of the terms of the trust (or a copy of the trust instrument); and (5) either a qualified appraisal or a detailed description of the method used to determine the fair market value of the property that was the subject of the gift.

14. IRC § 170A and Treasury regulations thereunder.

15. Treas. Reg. § 20.2031-6(b).

16. Internal Revenue Service, Art Appraisal Services, www.irs.gov/individuals/art-appraisal-services.

17. Rev. Proc. 96-15, 1996-3 I.R.B. 41.

18. For more on the Sonnabend estate, *see* Janet Novak, *The IRS Art Advisory Panel Has Its Head in the Clouds*, FORBES, July 22, 2012.

19. IRC § 6664(c)(1).

20. Estate of Kollsman v. Comm'r, T.C. Memo 2017-40 (2017).

21. Petition, Estate of Lisa de Kooning v. Comm'r, No. 004860-17 (T.C. Feb. 28, 2017).

5

Provenance

Everybody loves a good stolen art story (except when it involves their own art!). From the massive theft of art and other valuables systematically carried out by the Nazis during World War II, to the Gardner Museum heist in Boston, to the author's favorite, the theft of the Quedlinburg Treasures, hardly a week goes by that we do not read about some bold art heist—or recovery of stolen artwork—somewhere in the world.

But the topic of provenance goes far beyond the systematic looting by the Nazis and the bold deception of Joe Tom Meador (who stole the Quedlinburg Treasures). Today, the field of provenance goes beyond recovery of stolen art to include related concerns about authenticity and forgery, the chain of title to a particular piece, and competing claims that may arise over a piece of work. "Provenance" to collectors—"title" to lawyers—is critical to the planning process and actually to the broader practice of collecting art. In fact, many now describe this topic in broader terms: "provenance, authenticity, and good title."

Most assets have some form of ownership documentation—deeds for real estate, certificates of title for automobiles, account statements for securities—but most forms of tangible personal property do not. That holds true for most art, though, increasingly, there are registries that provide some evidence of ownership. Collectors are mostly left to build their own files on ownership, including certificates of authenticity, bills of sale, import and export documents, correspondence, insurance records, and perhaps affidavits from prior owners. Otherwise, the old adages of "possession is nine-tenths of the law" and "finders keepers, losers weepers" become more than playground taunts.

Until fairly recently—the last generation or so—most people in the art world did not pay particular attention to questions of provenance. It you possessed it, it was pretty much assumed that you owned it.

That all changed when the massive amount of artwork stolen in the years leading up to and during World War II started showing up at auction—and ancestors of the rightful owners started showing up as well! Imagine you bought an expensive piece of art at auction and the next day someone showed up with a picture of her grandmother's dining room in 1935 Berlin—and your recently acquired masterpiece was hanging on the wall. Worse yet would be the granddaughter's request that you give her the painting or that you write her a check for the same amount you just paid for the painting. That general fact pattern is now referred to as the "Restitution Cases," and all major auction houses employ experts in the field of provenance to guard against this problem.[1]

Stolen art is not limited to the ravages of World War II. Many readers will, of course, be familiar with the audacious 1990 art heist from the Gardner Museum in Boston—perhaps the largest art heist in American history in terms of dollar value. In the early morning hours of March 18, 1990, two thieves disguised as Boston police officers gained entry to the museum and stole 13 works of art:

- *The Concert* by Vermeer (one of only 34 known works by Vermeer in the world), which has been described as "the best painting in the world";
- *A Lady and Gentleman in Black* by Rembrandt;
- *The Storm on the Sea of Galilee* by Rembrandt (the artist's only known seascape);
- *Self-Portrait* by Rembrandt (postage-stamp-sized);
- *Landscape with Obelisk* by Govaert Flinck (formerly attributed to Rembrandt);
- *Chez Tortoni* by Manet;
- An ancient Chinese Ku from the Shang Dynasty;
- A finial in the shape of an eagle from a Napoleonic flag; and

- Five drawings by Degas:
  - ~ *La Sortie de Pesage*
  - ~ *Cortege aux Environs de Florence*
  - ~ *Program for an artistic soiree 1 & 2*
  - ~ *Three Mounted Jockeys*

All together, the stolen pieces are estimated to be worth over $500 million, making the robbery the largest private property theft in history. Several empty frames still hang in the museum's Dutch Room gallery, both in homage to the missing art and as placeholders if and when the pieces are returned.

The museum is still offering a reward of up to $10 million for information leading to the recovery of the stolen artwork even though the statute of limitations for prosecution of the crime has expired. The FBI has issued several press releases to the effect that it believes it knows the identity of the thieves and that the theft was carried out by a criminal organization based in the mid-Atlantic and New England regions. The FBI believes some of the art may have been sold in Philadelphia in the early 2000s.

The theft has become part of popular culture. The theft is the subject of a 2006 documentary called *Stolen* and has been featured on Court TV and the crime shows *American Greed* and *The Blacklist*. The Vermeer work even made its way into the art collection of Mr. Burns, Homer Simpson's greedy boss on *The Simpsons*. One or more of the pieces have been featured in several other movies and novels, usually possessed by a villain who is attempting to sell the art. But despite these appearances in popular culture, and rumors as to the location of the art, all 13 pieces are still missing.[2]

And the stories go on. It is said that Napoleon was the greatest art thief in history, as his armies looted the treasures of countries that he conquered. We all remember the famous image of Saddam Hussein's statue being toppled when his corrupt regime was ousted from Iraq. What we did not see was that as that famous image was being shown around the world, the museums of Baghdad were being looted. Even more recently, the Islamic State (commonly referred to as ISIS) and other terrorist organizations have routinely looted and sold antiquities to pay for a portion of their operations. And even the U.S. government got into the act when the now famous Monuments Men, tasked with rescuing art treasures when the Allied forces reclaimed conquered Europe in 1944 and 1945, were themselves ordered to pack up the best of the art and ship it home to the United States. These works were displayed at the State Department until President Eisenhower took office and ordered that it be shipped back to its rightful owners in Europe. It should be noted that the Monuments Men protested the original order.

The author's favorite stolen art story involves one Joe Tom Meador, from the little grain-farming community of Whitewright, Texas, 60 miles north of Dallas. Joe Tom, an obsessive-compulsive kleptomaniac, served with the 87th Armored Field Artillery Battalion, which landed at Normandy Beach on D-Day Plus One. As the 87th advanced across France and Germany, Joe Tom stole his way across France and Germany, packing and shipping his war booty back home.

Quedlinburg, Germany, had long been a favorite haunt of the Saxon and German kings, who brought gifts when they visited the cathedral. Over the years, these became known as the Quedlinburg Treasury and included many religious antiquities. On April 19, 1945, when the 87th rolled into Quedlinburg, the Treasury had been removed from the cathedral by the townspeople; some say the removal was to prevent it from being stolen by the Nazis who were still active in the area, and others claim it was to protect it from the bombing of the ever-advancing Allied forces. In either case, Joe Tom was one of the Allied soldiers tasked with protecting the Treasury from the Nazis. But Joe Tom had different ideas and instead stole 12 pieces himself, sending them home through the U.S. Army mail.

Shortly thereafter, Quedlinburg fell behind the Iron Curtain, and not much was heard about the Treasury. All assumed that the items had been destroyed or otherwise lost for all time.

Joe Tom went home to Whitewright, where he lived until his death in 1980. His sister, Ruth, who was executrix of his estate, filed a probate inventory and Texas inheritance tax forms but did not file a federal estate tax return or mention the Quedlinburg Treasures anywhere—even though, as it turns out, it was tucked away in a couple of safe deposit boxes at the First National Bank of Whitewright.

Three years later, in 1983, a somewhat comedic seven-year odyssey started, as Joe Tom's brother and sister tried to sell the Quedlinburg pieces through both legitimate and somewhat questionable avenues. They were quickly advised that what they had was the long-missing Quedlinburg pieces, which caused them to go underground.

A word about those underground markets. The art market itself is said to be the largest unregulated market in the world. And the stolen art market is reputed to be the third-largest illegal market in the world, behind only illegal drugs and guns.

In 1990, a press conference was held in Switzerland, where it was announced that a $3 million finder's fee was paid to recover one of the pieces, known as the *Samuel Gospels*, a manuscript written in golden ink, dating to the ninth century. By that time, word had spread that the rest of the Treasures were in Whitewright, and the Quedlinburg Cathedral sued the Meador siblings in federal district court in Dallas to recover the remaining Treasures. The parties settled, with the Meadors receiving a reported $2 million in return for the remaining Treasures.

But the story does not end there. The remaining Treasures went on display for six months at the Dallas Museum of Art before returning home. Problem was, the Treasures were two pieces short, and nobody, at least publicly, knows where they are.

Then the U.S. government indicted the Meadors for attempting to deal in stolen art in international commerce, which could have cost them 10 years in prison and a hefty fine. But alas, the indictment was filed one day late, one day after the statute of limitations had run out.

Finally, as if a civil lawsuit and a federal indictment were not enough for the Meadors, the IRS got into the act, pointing out that no federal estate tax return had been filed and that taxes, plus interest and penalty, were now approaching $50 million! It is reported that the assessment was settled for something in the range of $100,000.[3]

The lesson from this—besides don't steal art—is that there is a lot of stolen art out there.

My advice to a collector is that the farther away the collector is from the creator of the art and the older the art is, the more the collector should be concerned about provenance.

A collector who wants to research provenance before purchasing a work has several resources available, none of them completely foolproof. First, the FBI maintains the National Stolen Art File, a database of stolen artwork as reported to the FBI by law enforcement agencies throughout the world. At least two other databases are maintained—the Commission for Art Recovery, which lists items that are still missing from World War II, and the Art Loss Register, which is maintained by insurance companies and the art industry. The latter database allows you to register any art that has been stolen from you and also allows you to check the database to research whether a piece you are considering for purchase has been reported as stolen. Remember that these databases are limited to items known to have been stolen and reported to authorities.[4]

Although everyone loves a good stolen art story, this issue of provenance goes way beyond stolen art. Questions arise as to "title" of artwork every day—whether art was given or loaned to a family member, business partner, or special friend or donated or loaned to a museum; whether a consortium of galleries formed to represent an artist retains an interest in works subsequently sold; whether lenders who loaned money collateralized by certain works of art retain an interest; and so on and so forth. In short, every title claim that you can imagine can be, and has been, asserted against ownership of particular works of art and collections as a whole.

There are several companies that offer "title insurance" to help protect against losses. The author does not take a position as to whether collectors should purchase title insurance for their art. However, using a company such as this will mean that someone is assisting you in determining provenance before you purchase a particular piece and will be standing with you if a claim is subsequently made to recover the art. In addition, one company's website allows you to register to receive periodic alerts as to issues of provenance.[5]

Is It Real?

An area of increasing concern is authenticity: Is the piece of art you just bought real, or is it a copy? And if it is a copy, is it an authorized copy, or is it a forgery?

Case Study

Not long ago I was meeting with a collector. He is a world-renowned collector. I could not help but notice, and admire, the beautiful oil painting that hung behind his desk. He noticed my admiration and commented, "You know, that's not real." Well, certainly, it was real—I was looking at it! "No, I mean it's not the original. I own the original, but it is too valuable to hang in my office. But it is also too pretty to keep in storage. So I hired an artist to make a copy. The original is in storage; you are looking at the copy."

But go a step further. What if he (or his heirs) decided to sell the copy, passing it off as the original? Without expert help, I would not know the difference.

Counterfeit art has been around almost as long as art itself. There are certainly legitimate copies. There are even "copies" painted by the artist, simply the same scene painted more than once.

But rising art prices and the increasingly speculative approach taken by some collectors have combined to create a situation where the payoff to forgers has increased dramatically. And with the rise in the number of forgeries comes the rise in the number of lawsuits when forgeries are discovered.

For example, in 2011, one of the oldest galleries in America, Knoedler, was forced to close its doors after allegations that its former president had sold inauthentic works attributed to Jackson Pollock, Richard Diebenkorn, and others.[6]

Finally, remember that provenance is important not only to the collector but also to subsequent owners of the art, whether it is sold, passed by gift or inheritance, or donated to charity, all of which are discussed below. Establishing provenance will be much easier for your personal representatives or family members if you as the collector have maintained good records and an inventory of the collection.

Notes

1. Numerous books have been written about the systematic looting of European art by the Nazis. One of the best known is LYNN H. NICHOLAS, THE RAPE OF EUROPA: THE FATE OF EUROPE'S TREASURES IN THE THIRD REICH AND THE SECOND WORLD WAR (Vintage Press 1995).

2. For more on the Gardner robbery, readers may wish to read ULRICH BOSER, THE GARDNER HEIST: THE TRUE STORY OF THE WORLD'S LARGEST UNSOLVED ART THEFT (Harper 2010) or visit the FBI's website, http://www.fbi.gov.

3. For more on the Quedlinburg Treasures, readers may wish to read WILLIAM H. HONAN, TREASURE HUNT: A NEW YORK TIMES REPORTER TRACKS THE QUEDLINBURG HOARD (Fromm International 1993).

4. Art Loss Register, http://www.artloss.com.

5. Aris, http://www.aristitle.com.

6. Richard M. Horwood, *Key Issues for Collectors: Ownership, Authenticity, and Provenance*, 12 FAM. FOUND. ADVISOR, no. 3, Mar./Apr. 2013.

6

Liquidity

Art, by its very nature, is an illiquid asset. Certainly, it can be sold, by private sale or through public auction. But it is not like cash or publicly traded stocks or bonds that can be quickly converted to cash through public, mostly efficient, transparent markets. Furthermore, a sale will cause recognition of gain for any appreciation in the art, triggering federal income tax as high as 31.8 percent, plus any applicable state income tax. Finally, art does not produce a regular stream of income.

From a planning perspective, the illiquid nature of art, as with any illiquid asset, provides certain planning opportunities but also planning challenges. Those planning opportunities and challenges are discussed in chapters 7 through 14.

Apart from dispositive planning, the illiquidity of art presents challenges both during the collector's lifetime and at death. During life, the collection may represent a significant portion of the collector's wealth, without producing regular income or capital for other uses, which may or may not present a problem for a particular collector, depending on their other resources. Significant noncharitable transfers during life may require the payment of federal gift taxes. At death, in addition to possible federal estate taxes, there will be significant estate administration expenses associated with storing, insuring, and carrying out other risk-management activities related to the art, as well as costs associated with owning, maintaining, and disposing of a collection. Furthermore, depending on the ultimate disposition of the collection, the estate may require liquidity to equalize distributions if an unequal distribution of the collection is planned.

In short, not only may art be expensive to acquire, but also it is expensive to maintain and expensive to dispose of.

Art Lending

Although most collectors acquire art for aesthetic reasons, to enjoy and display, over time a collection may come to represent significant value, which may carry with it significant expense to properly maintain. For a variety of reasons, a collector may wish to access the value represented by the collection, without selling any of the pieces. Reasons to access the wealth may include maintaining a certain lifestyle, acquiring more art, or pursuing other business ventures or investments. In short, their collection may represent a significant amount of wealth, and the collector may wish to unlock that capital for other uses without incurring taxes and expenses associated with a sale.

Certain financial firms and private banks have long offered their qualifying clients loans secured by valuable works of art. This has been especially true in the recent past as the value of art in general has grown significantly, more high-net-worth individuals have acquired art, and art markets have become a bit more transparent than in the past. At the same time, more and more financial firms have seen the opportunity to increase their asset-backed loan portfolios by making loans collateralized by art.

Case Study

A collector was also a real estate developer with a long track record of developing large condominium projects. Several years ago, with the overall economy still in recovery from the worst financial crisis in decades, real estate construction financing was virtually impossible to obtain—and then only on less than desirable terms. The collector did not want to sell other assets, including his collection, triggering capital gains tax, to secure liquidity for a new project.

The collector was instead able to use a portion of his art collection to secure a line of credit to allow him to proceed with a new project. The loan was structured so that all of the art remained in the collector's possession, to display or loan to museums, as he wished. Furthermore, this type of loan is much easier to document and much faster to close than a real estate construction loan.

Several other case studies involving art lending are included in chapter 15.

Loan details will, of course, vary, as so-called art loans are individually negotiated. Here are some of the terms that should be taken into consideration when contemplating an art loan:

Amount. This will vary by lender. However, most art loans will be in excess of $1 million.

Structure. Most art loans will be structured as a renewable line of credit.

Pricing. The interest rate will typically be variable, or floating, based on a spread over the 30-day BBA LIBOR index rate.

Advance. This is typically up to 50 percent of the appraised value of the art serving as collateral.

Collateral. Typically, the collector will maintain possession of the art, with a security interest granted by the collector to the lender, perfected by the filing of a UCC-1 Financing Statement. This allows the collector to continue to display their collection or even lend it to museums, as long as the lender is kept aware of the art's location. Although some lenders may loan against individual pieces, it is more common for a collection, or portion of a collection, to be used as collateral to secure the loan. Also, not all art is acceptable by lenders. Again, this may vary by lender, but diversified collections of old masters, modern art, impressionists, postwar contemporary, and Asian and American artists are more readily accepted. Some lenders may loan on other forms of art and other categories of collectibles.

Appraisals. Appraisals will be required, likely with annual updates.

Provenance. As discussed in chapter 5, provenance is critical and must be documented through a bill of sale and affidavit of ownership.

Recourse. Loans will typically provide full recourse; that is, the borrower will remain personally liable for repayment of the loan. There are some lenders that will make nonrecourse loans, meaning that the borrower will not have personal liability beyond the collateral posted to secure the loan. These loans will likely bear a higher rate of interest to reflect the increased risk being taken by the lender.

Lenders generally do not look to the sale of the art for repayment but rather will require that the collector have another source of repayment. If the art is legally owned by an entity such as a limited liability company, the collector will be required to guarantee the loan. The collector will also be required to carry insurance equal to the appraised value, with the lender as a named loss payee.[1]

Taxes and Related Expenses

If the collector determines to make gifts of art to family members or other noncharitable donees, then, as discussed in chapter 10, any gifts above the AEA will require that the collector pay federal gift taxes. These are due and must be paid by the due date of Form 709, Federal Gift Tax Return, generally at the same time as Form 1040, Federal Income Tax Return, for the year in question. This is true whether the gift is the art itself or an entity that owns the art, such as a limited liability company.

To the extent that the collector dies owning the art and the value is such that an estate tax is due (federal and/or state), that estate tax must be paid within nine months of the date of death even if the filing deadline for the estate tax return itself is extended.

In either case, when transferring an asset of potentially tremendous value but without corresponding liquidity (absent a sale), another source of assets must be used to pay the taxes due.

Beyond any transfer tax liability, other situations arise that may require additional liquidity.

A donation to charity generally gives rise to a federal income tax charitable deduction for the full value of the gift (during life) or bequest (at death), meaning that no gift tax liability or estate tax liability will be incurred for a qualifying charitable gift. However, it is not uncommon that a museum or other appropriate charity named to receive a collection will expect a cash gift to accompany the art, to provide for an endowment to support the continued curation of the collection and the museum where it is housed.

During the period of estate administration, as discussed in chapter 12, costs of maintaining and insuring the collection may be significant. And beyond estate administration, the collector must consider the resources of the eventual recipient of their collection and whether the collector will need to leave them other assets sufficient to ensure their ability to maintain the collection.

All of these "expenses" must be considered in the planning process.

Estate Equalization

A collection may comprise a significant portion of the value of the estate. This can pose issues when less than all family members have an interest in the art, yet all want "their" share of the value.

For example, a collector wishes to leave her collection to her daughter and her other assets to her son. At the same time, the collector wants them each to receive more or less equal value. Assume we are dealing with a taxable estate. In that case, the government always wants its share as well; in fact, it insists on it!

Any planning will need to take into account the need for liquidity to pay estate taxes and perhaps also the need for liquidity to "equalize" the inheritance. Specific examples of this are given in chapter 15.

In summary, one of the greatest challenges of owning art is its illiquid nature, which must be taken into account in the planning process.

Note

1. Jose E. Sirven & Liliana M. Vidal, *The Art of Lending on Art*, ABA BANKING J., May 11, 2012.

PART 3

Planning

Art is a unique asset. It is an asset of passion but also an asset
that is expensive to own. It is also illiquid and does not produce
current income. Combined, these characteristics present both technical and personal planning challenges.

7

The Process

For collectors concerned with the seemingly endless choices about what to do with their art, I point out that they really have only three choices: sell it, give it to family (or other noncharitable beneficiary), or donate it to a charitable beneficiary. And there are really only two times they can do this: when they are alive and when they are not.

Three times two equals six . . . and that is how many options they have. These options are not mutually exclusive; in fact, it is common that a collector will use more than one planning option. However, these options are exhaustive—there are no others. We are not like the Egyptian pharaohs who "took it with them." And much to their chagrin, even that did not work in the end, given tomb robbers and more legitimate archeological excavations!

Unless, of course, the collector selects the default option, which is to do nothing. Now, doing nothing may be the right choice, unlikely though it may be. But even if doing nothing is the right choice, I prefer for it to be an educated choice.

Another so-called option to avoid is sometimes called the "moving van" option or, in the case of art, the "empty hook" option. This option, not limited to art or other collectibles, counts on the family or others removing the property from the collector's home and not reporting it on the federal estate tax return or otherwise as a taxable transfer. This approach is illegal. Furthermore, the IRS was not born yesterday. Although it is somewhat limited in resources to conduct full-blown, on-site audits,

Form 706, Estate Tax Return, will give hints as to whether an appropriate amount of tangible personal property is reported on the return. And for well-known collectors and larger collections, the IRS may already be aware of the existence of art in the estate. An examiner will also routinely request insurance policies, which may reflect the ownership of art. Finally, for advisors, it is unethical to participate in taxable transfers that are not reported. So do not elect this option!

Setting aside the do-nothing option—which, by the way, is the favorite of probate litigation attorneys—let's explore the six real options available to a collector as they plan for the ultimate disposition of their collection:

- Sell during life is discussed in chapter 9;
- Gift, to family or other noncharitable beneficiaries, during life is discussed in chapter 10;
- Donate, to charity, during life is discussed in chapter 11;
- Sell at death is discussed in chapter 12;
- Bequeath, to family or other noncharitable beneficiaries, at death is discussed in chapter 13; and
- Donate, to charity, at death is discussed in chapter 14.

In chapter 15, a number of case studies are discussed. Finally, in chapter 16, I provide a "Top Ten" list of planning do's and don'ts.

A new part 5 addresses planning for artists, during life and after death, including the use of artist-funded foundations.

And finally, because so many books and articles have been written about art and its various related topics, I have included a list of other resources at the end of the book.

8

The Big Question

When we approach planning, we do need to get the hardest question out of the way first. And that is, Does your family want your art? And I do not mean the value of your art; I mean the art itself. As I like to say, there is a big difference between a $10 million painting and a painting worth $10 million. Do they like the art, or do they like the value of the art? The answer to this question will determine which of the planning options discussed below are appropriate.

Case Study

A collector owned approximately $20 million of art, all displayed in his home. He decided to give a portion of the collection to his children. His primary motive in planning this gift was to remove the art, and future appreciation on the art, from his estate. He also planned to retain possession of the art, which is a separate issue discussed in chapter 10.

It turns out that the collector had not asked his children the Big Question: Do you want my art? Discussing this with his advisors further, it turns out that he had not even considered the question, assuming that, of course, they would want his art—or certainly the value of the art. After a shorthand conversation about the six options, he reconsidered this planned gift of art. It seems that his objective was wealth-transfer planning, not planning with art, a distinction that I hope becomes clear to the reader of this book.

--- *Case Study* ---

A collector, with a collection of modern art worth approximately $2 million, has two adult daughters. In the course of planning, she was asked, "Do your daughters like the art?" Her response was that they were lukewarm about the art itself but they would each like at least one piece for sentimental reasons. Perhaps just as important, neither of the daughters had a lifestyle, professional or personal, conducive to collecting and displaying valuable art. Nothing improper or immoral—just that their financial circumstances and living arrangements were not conducive to owning art of this magnitude.

It was determined that the best course of action was to allow each of the daughters to select one piece from the collection and to leave the balance to a museum that already had several pieces donated by the collector.

That was not the end of the story, though. A host of questions needed to be resolved:

- Who selects the two pieces, the daughters themselves or their mother?
- When do they select and receive the pieces, now or at their mother's death?
- Does value matter? In other words, if one daughter selected a piece worth $5,000 and the other a piece worth $100,000, would there be an equalizing distribution? And would that equalizing distribution affect either daughter's choice?

The collector should also have a discussion with the museum about her donation to them. She should ask:

- Will my collection stay intact and separate, or will it become part of the museum's general collection?
- Will there be a minimal amount of display time? Most collectors want their works to be on display, not in the basement in storage.
- Will you loan the collection? Will you sell the collection?
- Will you require that additional funds be donated to support the cost of maintaining the collection?

These are all questions that a collector and a museum should discuss before a donation agreement is made.

This collector chose to have these discussions up front, with her family and with the museum. That is the preferred method, although one could choose to simply leave instructions in the will.

A Word About "Family"

When I talk about "family," I am using the term collectively and broadly. It could be that some family members love the art as much as the collector does, while others do not. That is okay and needs to be addressed as part of the larger wealth-transfer planning process. Usually, there are ways to deal with it. It is similar to owning a family business where some of the next generation will be involved and others will not be involved. Most people want some sort of equality of distribution, and that can most often be dealt with by using other assets or life insurance (if reasonably available).

So the question is, Does the family care about the art? If not, then that will likely lead to a sale or a donation to charity, both discussed below. If they do love the art, then it will likely call for a wealth-transfer solution, either during life or at death.

When I use the term "family," I really mean natural persons rather than a charity. *Leave It to Beaver* households still exist but are far from the norm these days. I will use the terms "family," "children," "grandchildren," and so on, but this really means any noncharitable beneficiary. Likewise, the term "spouse" has a new meaning today. There is still some uncertainty in the area of tax planning for same-sex couples, which is often state dependent, so they should take particular care when planning.

If the family does like the art (as opposed to just the value of the art), then some of the wealth-transfer techniques discussed below will be appropriate. If the family cares only for the wealth represented by the art, then other solutions are called for. The challenge is knowing which they care for, and this discussion can be a delicate one.

And here is where collectors often get a big surprise. They have an incredible passion for their collections and assume that everyone else, especially their family members, shares that passion and appreciation. Well, that is not necessarily the case, and more often than not, the family does not share that passion; in fact, quite often family members resent the time, attention, and financial resources that have been lavished on the art instead of them.

It is also possible that the family members do not yet know if they have the same passion for the collection.

Case Study

A collector started his collection in earnest just a few years ago. He had always had an interest in the type of art that he collects, but he was not able to pursue it fully until a liquidity event that occurred several years earlier. The collection has since grown by some order of magnitude, both in the number and quality of pieces and in the value of the collection.

The collector's children, and their spouses, all appreciate the beauty of the art, but they are busy raising young children and building careers. They honestly do not know yet how all of this may fit into their lives. So for the time being, no permanent plans are being made for the collection beyond a general disposition in the will. This allows the collector to maintain options with respect to where the collection might ultimately go, depending on how the family's interest progresses.

In summary, the Big Question must be asked. Do not be surprised by the answer. But do understand that the answer to the Big Question is the driver behind the rest of the planning process.

9

Selling—During Life

Before we discuss the planning options, it is important to note that it is imperative to properly document any transfers. It is amazing to the author how many large-dollar transactions are completed with nothing more than a bill of sale and a check or, worse, just a handshake and a check! Whatever formalities are required, do not be penny-wise and pound-foolish . . . make sure the documents are done correctly by top-notch attorneys, not glossed over to save a little money on attorney or other transaction fees. And make sure that any transaction is reflected on your inventory and any insurance policies and, where required, appropriately documented to taxing authorities.

Selling your collection—in whole or in part—may be the right choice for you, but you should be aware that art and other collectibles are perhaps not only the most expensive assets that you will ever buy but also the most expensive assets that you will ever sell.

To understand the income tax treatment for sales of art, it is first necessary to determine into which category of taxpayer you fall. Owners of art fall into one of four categories—artists, collectors, investors, or dealers, as defined in chapter 1.

For collectors and investors, art is a capital asset. If it has been owned for a year or less, then any gain on sale will be subject to federal income tax at ordinary income tax rates. If it has been held for over one year—a year and a day—it is a long-term capital asset. For several years, we were used to thinking of the top federal income tax rate on long-term capital gains as being 15 percent. That is still true for most long-term capital assets and for most taxpayers, though higher-income taxpayers (over $479,000 in adjusted gross income in 2018 for married taxpayers filing jointly) now pay at a top long-term capital gain rate of 20 percent.

But that is not true for art—or other collectibles. Collectibles are defined in IRC § 408(m) to include "any work of art, any rug or antique, any metal or gem, any stamp or coin, any alcoholic beverage, or any other tangible personal property specified by the Secretary of the Treasury for such purposes."[1] The federal long-term capital gains tax rate for collectibles is as high as 28 percent of the amount of gain realized upon sale.

Also, since 2013, again for collectors and investors but not for artists and dealers, the health-care surtax of 3.8 percent applies to net investment income above certain amounts. This includes gain from the sale of art, so that the top federal income tax rate on long-term capital gain realized from the sale of art is 31.8 percent.

Add to the federal income tax cost the myriad transaction costs applicable to sellers of art, regardless of tax classification—which may include the seller's commissions; state income taxes (if any); packaging, transportation, and storage; and insurance—and the total cost of selling appreciated works of art climbs. Hence, my earlier statement that art may be the most expensive asset that a collector ever sells!

That does not mean that selling is not the right option—it just means that the collector who sells during life will incur significant expenses in doing so.

Art of the Deal(er)

The long-term capital gains rate and the 3.8 percent surtax apply to collectors and investors but not to artists and dealers in art or other collectibles. For artists and dealers, art is inventory, and gains on the sale of inventory are subject to tax at ordinary income tax rates (though the health-care surtax does not apply). It is certainly possible, and actually quite common, for artists and dealers to have their own collections separate and apart from their inventory. Both should be careful to maintain records of their separate collections, as they will qualify as collectors or investors for such pieces. And it is possible that various pieces of art may move from one category to another over time.

Movin' on Up

For investors, but not for artists, collectors, or dealers, it was possible (and quite common) to "trade up" by entering into a "like-kind" exchange under section 1031 of the IRC.[2] Like-kind exchanges are no longer permitted for any asset other than certain real estate; therefore, like-kind exchanges are no longer permitted for art or other collectibles for any class of taxpayer.

Prior to 2018, when like-kind exchanges were still permissible for art and other collectibles, the question for collectors was, Can I become an investor and take advantage of like-kind exchange treatment? The answer was fact dependent.

That question is no longer relevant. Instead, the question is, Can a collector/investor become a dealer and, even though they are subject to ordinary income tax rates (up to 37 percent on the federal level) that are higher than capital gains rates (combined, 31.8 percent on the federal level), also qualify for the new 20 percent qualified business income ("QBI") deduction available under IRC § 199A in certain circumstances? If so, then the effective top federal income tax rate drops to 29.6 percent (37 percent times 80 percent to take the QBI deduction into account). This is a reduction in the top rate of 2.2 percent (29.6 versus 31.8 percent).

Again, this will be a fact-dependent determination, but it is unlikely that many collectors/investors in art will be able to qualify for the QBI deduction unless they can demonstrate that they are engaged in a legitimate, active trade or business.

The consequences for attempting, but failing, to qualify for such treatment are twofold. First, if collectors/investors fail to demonstrate qualification for that tax classification, they will be subject to an even higher top federal tax rate (37 versus 31.8 percent). Furthermore, they may be subject to income tax underpayment penalties, which are twice as high for QBI miscalculations as for other types of underpayments.

Another temptation will be to transfer art to a C corporation, which now has a top federal income tax rate of 21 percent—quite attractive when compared to the higher combined federal long-term capital gains rate of 31.8 percent. Again, the problem is twofold. First, if one collected art through a C corporation, sales would be taxed at the federal rate of 21 percent, but then proceeds left in the C corporation would be exposed to the accumulated earnings tax and/or the personal holding company tax, and proceeds distributed would be subject to dividend taxation, the latter resulting in a federal combined top rate of 44.8 percent, the highest rate of all of these alternatives. Further, if the art is owned by the C corporation but displayed in the owner's home, that could be deemed to be a distribution of corporation assets, better known as a dividend and taxable as such. A case that involved just that situation appears in chapter 10 in the discussion of estate planning.

The lesson is that each collector has their own set of facts, and projections need to be prepared in each case before making any such changes in legal structure or tax classification.

Does Art Always Increase in Value?

Of course not! But just like other investments, no one talks about their losers, only their winners. Coupled with the astronomical prices paid at auction in recent years for pieces such as those mentioned in chapter 2, one would think that art is a "sure thing." Hence, most discussions about art assume that the piece being sold has appreciated.

But it is possible that a piece has lost value and the collector has incurred a capital loss. Losses from capital assets are netted against gains in the normal capital gain/loss netting process. A net capital loss is limited to $3,000 per year, applied against ordinary income.

Should I Be a Dealer Instead?

It is common for collectors to travel to art shows and art fairs across the country and even around the world. In some cases, collectors have been known to "reclassify" themselves as dealers and to treat their travel expenses as expenses incurred in a trade or business, deductible under section 162. To the extent that facts and circumstances are such that a collector could be deemed to be a dealer, thereby allowing reasonable and necessary expenses incurred in a trade or business to be deducted, the trade-off, of course, is that any sales of art would be sales of inventory, taxable as ordinary income. This scenario is fact dependent, both as to its legitimacy and as to whether the tax treatment works in the taxpayer's favor or not—I have heard arguments both ways.

The question of whether an investor can or should become a dealer has taken on a different importance starting in 2018, since like-kind exchanges are no longer available for art transactions. The discussion immediately above under "Movin' on Up" is germane to this decision.

How Do I Go About Selling a Piece or a Collection?

One thing I have learned is that collectors are not generally sellers. However, the time may come when a collector decides to sell one or more pieces or the family or personal representatives of the collector's estate decide to sell one of more pieces. This may even occur in the context of a charitable disposition where a decision is made to sell a piece and then donate the proceeds to charity or where pieces are left to a private foundation with the intent that the foundation should sell the pieces and use the proceeds for its charitable mission. Although the collector is generally aware of the sales process, having been on the other side so often, it may be that the collector's family, personal representatives, and advisors are not.

There are myriad ways to sell art. Most art sales that we hear about occur at public auctions. Yet more art is sold in private transactions than through public auctions. This, of course, includes sales to collectors by galleries, dealers, and artists themselves. And today, it is possible to list your art online, either through such online sellers as eBay or through auction houses that increasingly conduct auctions online simultaneously with live auctions. And many of these sales are composed of items consigned from estates.

There are two basic ways to go about selling individual pieces or collections as a whole: public sales through auction houses and private sales through dealers.

Collectors are, of course, familiar with auctions and likely have attended many auctions throughout the course of their collecting career. Most of the time, though, they are there to buy, not sell, so the following focuses on the auction process from the selling, or consignment, side. The main benefit of selling through auction is that the art is potentially exposed to a broader market than with a private sale, thereby at least theoretically bringing the best price. However, there is the possibility that an item will not sell, which may affect its perceived value in the future. Auctions are also run according to the auction houses' calendars, meaning that a significant time period may be involved between consignment and receipt of proceeds. Finally, auctions are public affairs, and collectors or their families, personal representatives, or advisors may wish for a sale to remain private for a number of reasons.

First, the collector or other seller who desires to sell art at auction needs to identify which auction house to use. These can range from the internationally known auction houses such as Christie's, Sotheby's, Philips, Bonhams, and Heritage Auctions to more regional and local auction houses. Different auction houses have different specialties and varying degrees of exposure. The collector or other seller needs to interview the auction house to determine if its expertise is compatible with the collector's pieces. They need to ask about past auctions and review its catalogs to determine if the auction house will be able to give maximum exposure to the art they plan to sell.

The auction house will in turn want to know exactly what the collector wants to sell and will want to examine images of the pieces, if not the pieces themselves, to determine condition. Evidence of provenance will need to be provided. At this point, the auction house can determine if it is interested in selling these particular items; if not, the auction house may be able to recommend another auction house, online auction, or nonauction market outlet.

At the point that the auction house agrees to accept the items for consignment and the items are shipped to the auction house, the auction house will establish an auction estimate for each item, which is the range of values that the auction house expects the item will sell for. This will take into account the condition of the piece, current market conditions, past auction results, and similar factors.

Packaging and shipping costs, as well as insurance costs, are usually the responsibility of the collector, though different auction houses may bear a portion or all of the insurance costs while items are in their possession. This is another point of discussion when selecting an auction house.

usually a seller's commission applies .

Once an item is placed into auction and is sold, the collector will incur costs associated with the sale, most notably a seller's commission. This will likely be a percentage of the sales price. The percentage amount will vary by auction house and by the category of item being sold. For example, the seller's commission on art will likely be different than that for other collectibles, such as coins or antique furniture. In addition, the auction house may charge a set fee, either a dollar amount or a percentage of the sales price, for photography, insurance, and marketing of the item. Although the amount may appear to be small, it may equal a significant amount if the collector, or collector's estate, is selling a large collection with multiple pieces. Keep in mind that depending on the collector and the collection, the selling commission may be negotiable, whereas the buyer's commission, discussed below, generally is not negotiable.

It may take 6 to 12 months from initial consignment until an auction occurs and final settlement is made. As a result, some auction houses may allow an advance of a certain amount of the expected sales proceeds. The availability of this option varies by auction house and will also depend on the number and value of the items being sold. It is common for the advance to carry a finance charge. As practices vary greatly, this should be discussed when selecting an auction house if this is of importance to the collector.

Most auction houses are expert marketers. After all, they are in the business of selling art and other collectibles, and they generally produce beautifully photographed catalogs, which include a detailed description, a condition evaluation, and the provenance of each item being sold. Part of the selection process should be to inquire as to the marketing plan for your items.

All of this leads, of course, to the auction itself. Collectors are generally aware of the auction process. The auction will usually be preceded by the mailing of the catalog for the auction to the auction house's contact list, designated on-site viewing hours, and, increasingly, the ability to view the auction lots online for some period of time prior to the official auction. This usually includes the opportunity for interested buyers to place bids in advance.

At the auction, bidders will appear in person, by telephone, and online. The auctioneer moves from lot to lot, starting at a previously announced starting bid and accepting bids until there is a clear-cut winner. There may be a minimum, or reserve, established beforehand, which may or may not be announced, and if the high bid does not reach that level, then the lot will be removed from the auction.

Once an item is sold, the buyer immediately becomes the legal owner of the item but generally cannot take physical possession until the purchase price is paid. The buyer will also usually pay a buyer's premium, which is a percentage of the sales price. This buyer's premium is often included in the announced winning bid price, so be aware that the prices that are announced publicly include this markup.

Finally, settlement can occur, and the collector receives the proceeds, net of the expenses incurred in the process.

One last matter about auctions should be considered, and that is the possibility that an item does not sell, either because there were no bids or no bids exceeded any reserve price. In such a case, the item may be returned to the collector, or it may be held for the next auction of similar items, usually with a lower reserve or estimate. The cost of this situation varies and should be addressed in discussions between the collector and the auction house.

The alternative to a sale through an auction house is a sale through a dealer or art gallery. Again, it is likely that a collector will have relationships with one or more dealers and will likely understand the process by which a dealer may sell their art. Similar to auctions, though, the family, personal representatives of the collector's estate, and advisors may not share that familiarity.

Most of us think of dealers and art galleries as a place to purchase art, and that is certainly true. However, it is also common to sell art through dealers. Advantages to using a dealer over an auction house include privacy and more control over the ultimate sale.

Dealers have expertise in the art that they sell, and through their network with other dealers and collectors, they are familiar with the art market. Certainly, they specialize, so it is important to work with a dealer who is familiar with the collector's particular art medium.

Selling through a dealer generally takes one of two forms—a direct sale to the dealer or a consignment sale.

With a direct sale to the dealer, the dealer buys directly from the collector. The advantage to this method is that the collector receives the proceeds immediately, and privately, unlike with a sale at auction. The potential disadvantage is that the dealer may pay less than a collector might receive at auction because the dealer will want to be able to mark the price up to make a profit on resale.

A consignment means that the collector delivers the art to the dealer, who then attempts to sell the art on behalf of the collector. A consignment agreement is entered into, which typically lasts for six months to one year. During that time, the dealer will attempt to sell the art, and proceeds will be split between the collector and dealer. Costs to make the art ready for sale, such as reframing and any needed restoration, will typically be borne by the collector, while the dealer will typically pay any costs of shipping and insurance.

In either case, whether selling at auction or through a dealer, it is imperative to have a well-crafted consignment agreement in place, to establish ownership of the art against any possible competing claims that may arise, and to define the rights and responsibilities of the owner of the art and the auction house or dealer.[3]

Summary

Selling a piece or an entire collection of art may be the right choice, but the collector (and advisors) must be aware that it might very well be the most expensive option from both a tax and an overall cost point of view.

Notes

1. IRC § 408.

2. Like-kind exchange treatment is governed by IRC § 1031.

3. Richard M. Horwood, *Key Issues for Collectors: Working with Dealers and Auction Houses*, 13 Fam. Found. Advisor, no. 1, Nov./Dec. 2013, includes an excellent discussion of considerations when selling art.

10

Gifting—During Life

Back to our initial question: Does your family share your passion for your collection? If not, then giving it to them during life or leaving it to them at death holds little appeal. And remember, we are talking about the collection or the individual pieces—we are not talking about the value represented by the collection or the individual pieces. That is wealth-transfer planning as opposed to planning with art.

Whether we are talking about wealth-transfer planning or planning with art, which techniques will be appropriate depends to a great extent on the balance of the estate. For those whose total estate is less than the federal AEA ($11,400,000 in 2019; indexed for inflation thereafter; twice that amount for a married couple), tax minimization will not be as important as it will be for those whose total estate exceeds that amount. Still, nontax considerations—those topics discussed in chapters 3 through 6—will be important.

Back to planning. Let's assume that one or more of your children, or other family members, or even special friends, do share your passion for your art. Perhaps this passion extends to the entire collection, perhaps only to some significant pieces. Again, we are talking about the art itself, not the value of the art, which is an entirely different thing. You might be tired of reading that, but I cannot overemphasize that point!

To put this into context, we should first understand the basics of the federal transfer tax system.[1] A gratuitous transfer—a gift during life or a bequest or other transfer at death—is subject to transfer taxes: gift tax if made during life and estate tax if made at death. If the transfer is to someone two or more generations down, then the transfer is subject to a second tax, the generation-skipping transfer tax, which is assessed in addition to the gift or estate tax. The tax rate for each of these taxes is, practically speaking, 40 percent of the value of the asset that is transferred.

There are exceptions to these taxes, and exceptions provide planning opportunities. First, anyone can give $15,000 each year to each of any number of people. That amount is indexed for inflation, increased in $1,000 increments. A married couple can double this amount, giving $30,000 each year to each of any number of people. For example, a married couple with two children and four grandchildren could give them a total of $180,000 each year without paying gift taxes or using any of their AEA. Properly structured, the gifts to the grandchildren would not be subject to the generation-skipping transfer tax or use any of the generation-skipping transfer tax exemption. Gift recipients are not limited to family members, though practically speaking, that is to whom we make gifts.

On top of this amount, everyone is entitled to make additional transfers of the AEA ($11.4 million, indexed for inflation). That amount can be used to make tax-free gifts during life, with any unused amount offsetting estate taxes at death.

For gifts two or more generations down, there is another tax, the generation-skipping transfer tax, which is imposed to carry out the fundamental federal tax policy that wealth transfers should be subject to the transfer tax system at least once each generation. This tax also has two exceptions: properly structured $15,000 annual gifts will not be subject to the tax, and there is an $11.4 million exemption from the tax, also indexed for inflation.

From a purely tax planning point of view, you can see that a significant amount of wealth, including art, can be transferred without incurring any federal transfer tax. The collector can use the $15,000 annual gift tax exclusion and larger AEA to transfer individual pieces or even make fractional gifts of larger pieces. As with other assets, these gifts may be made outright or made in trust. The use of a trust may provide additional benefits as well. First, the collector may keep a larger portion of the collection intact rather than breaking it into different pieces to keep the value of gifts under the annual exclusion amount. And depending on the makeup of the family, the trust could include generation-skipping provisions, which would allow the trust to remain intact for a longer period of time. The use of a trust structure is discussed further below, as it does provide some practical challenges.

Case Study

A collector has a net worth of approximately $30 million, including art recently appraised for insurance purposes at $15 million. The collector's two children both share her passion for contemporary art, and the entire family would like to see the art stay in the family for years to come. The collector decides to start transferring individual pieces to her children, using first the $15,000 annual gift tax exemption and, for pieces valued over that amount, a portion of her lifetime AEA. Over time, the collector will be able to transfer her entire collection to her children without paying any gift tax and will retain her financial assets for her own use. Financial assets will also be available for any federal estate tax that will be due at her death.

Where appropriate, more advanced gifting techniques, such as grantor-retained annuity trusts (GRATs), family limited partnerships (FLPs), limited liability companies (LLCs), and transactions using grantor trusts (defective as to the grantor or the beneficiary) may also be used. All of these are discussed below. Transfers involving charities and charitable trusts are discussed in chapter 11.

The primary transfer tax advantage to making gifts of art (or any asset for that matter) is that the value of the art is "frozen" for transfer tax purposes and any future appreciation in the art will not be includable in the collector's estate.

For example, let's say a collector gave a painting worth $1 million to her daughter. To keep it simple, let's say that the collector's estate will be subject to federal estate tax (that is, over the AEA), that the daughter loves art as much as her mother loves art, and further that the daughter has an appropriate home and other resources and understands the responsibility that goes along with owning art with significant value. Let's also assume that the mother gave her daughter $15,000 in cash, using the annual gift exclusion.

No gift tax would be due at the time of the gift of art because it is covered by—but counts against—the AEA.

Let's say the art doubled in value between the time of the gift and when the mother died. If the gift had not been made, then the original $1 million, plus the $1 million of appreciation, would be included in the collector's estate, subject to tax at 40 percent. But since the gift was made, although the $1 million value of the gift is considered when calculating estate taxes, the $1 million of appreciation is not. Again, keeping things simple, this saved the collector's family $400,000 in federal estate taxes, 40 percent of the amount of appreciation that occurred after the gift was made.

As we will see below, this transfer tax savings does not by itself mean you should rush out and give your art to your family!

Several important caveats and special considerations must be taken into account when attempting wealth transfer with art. And this is why it is critical to know if the family (defined expansively) cares about the art itself or the value of the art.

First, art is less liquid than many other assets. Although art certainly can be sold (see chapter 9 for considerations when selling art), gifting to the next generation is really done with the intent of keeping the art, not selling it. Since art does not produce a steady stream of cash flow, techniques such as a GRAT and a sale to an intentionally defective grantor trust (both discussed below), which work especially well with assets that produce cash flow, will not work as well with art.

Second, the donee of the art will receive the donor's cost basis in the art. That means that the appreciation that escapes federal estate taxation because of a lifetime gift will eventually be subject to federal income tax on the capital gain if and when sold by the donee. Therefore, it is necessary to compare the transfer tax savings to be achieved by the lifetime gift with potential capital gains tax that might be due, as the basis would be stepped up to fair market value if it passed through the collector's estate. In fact, for estates up to the AEA, where no transfer taxes will be due, from a combined tax point of view, it may be preferable to hold the art until death, when the basis will be increased, or stepped up, to fair market value, thereby avoiding future capital gains tax on the appreciation.

Third, "discounting" techniques have not historically worked well with art. What do I mean by "discounting"? For those unfamiliar with the technique, it starts primarily with two basic concepts. First, a fractional interest in an asset, such as a minority interest in a business, is worth less than its proportionate share of the whole. Second, an asset that is not freely transferable, by sale or otherwise, is illiquid and, therefore, worth less than it otherwise would be.

The simplest example that I use is to ask what someone would pay for a 10 percent interest in a $100 bill. The book value is $10. But since you do not have control over the $100 bill (the "minority interest" part) and since you cannot liquidate your position without forcing a partition action (the "illiquidity" part), your 10 percent interest is not worth $10 on the open market.

What is it worth? I do not know, and I need a professional appraiser to tell me what it is worth. But I do know it is worth less than $10.

This is not tax lawyer stuff; it is economic reality. And these "discounts" to book value are at the center of wealth-transfer planning for people with taxable estates. These are not discounts to fair market value; they actually are fair market value.

There are many types of "discounts." Similar to the "minority interest" discount is the "fractional interest" discount—a fraction of the whole is not worth its proportion of the whole. Again, this is economic reality, not tax lawyer fiction.

The primary way that these discounts are achieved in estate planning is through the use of an FLP/LLC type of structure. The senior generation transfers assets to the FLP/LLC in return for partnership interests in the FLP/LLC. The senior generation then transfers the FLP/LLC interests to future generations, outright or in trust, through gifts and possibly sales. Whatever the structure of the transfer, it is valued at less than book value to reflect the discounts as determined by professional appraisers.

This is very effective planning. Although it has conceded the concept of discounting, the IRS continues to challenge discount planning on a factual basis—and even more so when the asset involved is art. The IRS has long taken the position that art, even when transferred as a fractional gift or through an FLP/LLC structure, is not entitled to a discount from book or face value for gift or estate tax purposes. Until recently, the IRS has been largely successful when taking this position with art.

At first blush, collectors and their tax advisors may take issue with this. Why should art or other collectibles be treated differently from real estate or closely held businesses? Why should an FLP/LLC funded with art be treated differently from one funded with marketable securities? That is precisely what collectors and their advisors have argued in the few cases that have gone to court on this issue.

Actually, the IRS position is intellectually consistent. A taxpayer is not *required* to take a discount for a charitable donation of a fractional interest in artwork, so why, therefore, would the taxpayer be *entitled* to a discount when the recipient is an individual as opposed to charity? There are more technical reasons behind the IRS's thinking, but the practical reality is that it has fought, mostly successfully, against the discounting of gifts of art, be it directly or through one or more family entities.

The author is not advocating one position or the other here. Until recently, there had been two relevant court decisions, *Stone v. United States* and the trial court opinion in *Estate of Elkins v. Commissioner*, which resulted in 5 percent and 10 percent discounts, respectively. Those discounts are insignificant compared to what is available through careful and appropriate wealth-transfer planning with other asset categories.

In *Stone v. United States*, a federal district court in California ultimately allowed a 5 percent discount to an estate that owned an undivided 50 percent interest in 19 paintings that were left to family members. The estate claimed a 44 percent fractional interest discount; the IRS initially argued that no discount should be allowed but eventually conceded a 5 percent discount. Significantly, the court noted that there is virtually no market for fractional interests in art; rather, all of the fractional interest owners would be more likely to sell an entire work and then split the proceeds. The court also noted that the taxpayer's appraisal methodology was flawed. The court encouraged the taxpayer and the IRS to agree on an appropriate discount. They were unable to do so, and the court allowed the 5 percent discount to reflect the cost of a partition suit, which is the legal remedy available to an owner of an undivided fractional interest if less than all owners are willing to sell the property in question.

The *Stone* decision was affirmed on appeal to the Ninth Circuit Court of Appeals, again noting the failure of the taxpayer to carry its burden of proof.[2]

Likewise, in the more recent Tax Court case of *Estate of Elkins v. Commissioner*, the taxpayer asserted fractional interest discounts and further restrictions on the art in question to reduce the value of art transferred to family members. The estate claimed a 44 percent discount; the IRS took the position that no discount should be allowed.

Although the facts in *Elkins* differ from those in *Stone*, the Tax Court result is practically the same. The Tax Court, though acknowledging that a discount could be found if supported by the facts of the case, allowed only a 10 percent discount to reflect the cost of a partition action.[3]

Stone and the Tax Court opinion in *Elkins* stand for these propositions:

1. There is no market for sales of fractional interests in art; therefore, there are no market data to support an appraisal for a discount to fair market value for gifts of art or for bequests of art from estates.
2. This is no rental market for works of what I will call masterpiece art (as opposed to decorative art). Therefore, the use of leasebacks of art, after gifting to family members or even charities, is problematic in that a fair rental value cannot be determined with certainty. This technique is further discussed below.

Assuming that "discounting" is not available in the same manner as with other assets, then it follows that collectors must examine their goals. Do they want to accomplish effective wealth transfer? Or do they want to transfer the art in an effective manner? If the primary goal is wealth transfer, then they are better off using other assets that are more likely to be subject to a greater discount than art to accomplish wealth transfer. If the goal is to keep the collection largely or wholly intact and within the family who has expressed an interest in maintaining and preserving, and even perhaps expanding, the collection, then certain other planning techniques should be considered.

The Tax Court decision in *Elkins* was reversed on appeal to the Fifth Circuit Court of Appeals, which has historically been receptive to discount valuation planning techniques, resulting in an overwhelming taxpayer victory. The effect of the *Elkins* appellate ruling is that—at least for now and at least in the Fifth Circuit—fractional interest discounts are permissible for gifts of fractional interests in artwork, presumably both direct gifts and gifts made via FLP/LLC planning. For the Elkins estate, the result was an approximate 45 percent discount for fractional interests in 64 pieces of artwork owned by the estate.

The taxpayer-friendly decision of *Elkins* should be tempered by several considerations.

First, although it was unlikely to do so, the IRS could have further appealed the *Elkins* decision to the U.S. Supreme Court. *Stone* and *Elkins* differ to some extent, but they do present a conflict between federal circuits: the Fifth Circuit allowed a taxpayer-friendly 45 percent discount, based on substantial evidence presented by the taxpayer at trial, while the Ninth Circuit allowed only a 5 percent discount to reflect the cost of partitioning the artwork in question.

Second, even though the time period has passed for the IRS to file an appeal to the U.S. Supreme Court in *Elkins*, the IRS may maintain its "no discount" position but change its trial strategy in the future. In *Elkins*, the IRS chose not to present any evidence to support its position or any expert testimony as to an appropriate discount. It is unlikely that the IRS will follow that course in the future.

Third, although *Elkins* was a resounding taxpayer victory, this question must now be asked: If a taxpayer may discount a gift of a fractional interest of art to a *noncharitable* donee, *must* a taxpayer take a similar discount when donating a fractional interest of art to a *charitable* donee? That issue has not been presented to date, and viable arguments exist that a gift of a fractional interest within a family and a donation of a fractional interest to a qualifying charity are two entirely different transactions even if they involve the exact same type of asset.

The ultimate outcome in *Elkins* may determine the future course of planning for art and other collectibles, so readers are encouraged to consult with their advisors or otherwise confirm the status of this potentially landmark decision.

Before we examine the ways to make gifts of art, we should also keep in mind possibly the biggest drawback to making gifts of art during life. This is one of the most common questions that I am asked: May I give away the art but retain possession? The argument typically is that the collector wants to give the art away, but (1) the donees are minor children living in the same home as the collector, or (2) the donees do not have a lifestyle (physical space, adequate security) to display the art. I suspect that the real reason is that the collector does not really want to part with the art, tax laws be damned!

I am not as troubled by the former scenario as by the latter. For minor children, I suggest that, at a minimum, the piece could be hung in their room, with clear indication it now belongs to the child, and that insurance and the inventory reflect the change in ownership. However, even as frequently as I am asked this question, it is unlikely that a collector will display an expensive piece of work in the child's room. There is even some question as to whether a minor can legally own tangible personal property under state property law.

The second scenario is troubling. Not only does it not pass the generic smell test, but also a gift is not legally a gift until the donor transfers possession to the donee. Making a gift, but retaining possession of the art, likely runs afoul of section 2036, which would cause the gifted piece to be included in the collector's estate even if he or she had ostensibly given it away. Just as in art law generally, at least before all of the stolen art cases started up, possession can also be ten/tenths of the tax law!

Taking these factors into consideration, the amount of art that can be transferred without paying gift tax, within the limits of the annual and lifetime use of the AEA, is significant. These gifts may be made directly or in trust and, depending on value, may be of individual pieces, fractional interests, or entire collections. For most people, that level of planning may be sufficient, again assuming that the family shares the collector's interest in the art. But as the size, and value, of the collection increases, further planning may be appropriate.

Family Partnerships

Family limited partnerships or family limited liability companies, sometimes referred to as "Art LLCs" (collectively, I will refer to them as LLCs for convenience sake), make a great deal of sense for the family that wants to keep a collection at least largely intact—even if little or no discounting may be available for federal gift or estate tax purposes.

An LLC is an entity formed under state law that is usually treated as a partnership for federal tax purposes. To use an LLC, the collector simply transfers ownership of the collection to the LLC. This requires the drafting of both appropriate documents to form the LLC and a bill of sale/

assignment document to transfer the collection. The latter can be either a fairly general blanket assignment or (preferably) a more detailed document, specifically listing each of the major items in the collection with perhaps a blanket assignment of the smaller items that may be too numerous to list. This change in ownership should be noted on insurance policies and the collector's inventory. For significant pieces that may be listed on registries, the ownership change should be noted. In short, the transfer of ownership should be complete legally and for purposes of provenance.

At this point, the LLC owns the art, and the collector owns the LLC. What has happened is that legal title and beneficial ownership of the art have effectively been separated. The collector has, in effect, created his own planning currency, which he can gift or bequeath without affecting the ownership of the art itself.

The collector can now use the LLC to gift beneficial interests in the artwork/collection without regard to the actual title to specific pieces. The collection can be maintained by the managers of the LLC—initially, this would be the collector, but over time, other family members who are knowledgeable about the art may be added as managers. The managers are responsible for managing the collection, including maintaining insurance and making decisions regarding the display or even the sale of the art. The LLC may also lend the art to museums as appropriate.

For example, say the collector couple owns 60 pieces in their collection and has three children. Rather than giving each child 20 pieces of art, or a one-third fractional interest in all 60 paintings—a situation that is primed for conflict—the paintings would be contributed to an LLC. Depending on value, either all at once or over a period of time each child would receive a one-third interest in the LLC. If the managers of the LLC (the collectors during their lives, the children and grandchildren after that) decided to sell certain of the paintings, the proceeds could be either distributed to the children and grandchildren or retained and reinvested in other artwork. If fewer than all family members wanted to participate in the future of the collection, perhaps gifts of other assets could be made to them to equalize the ultimate estate distribution.

Finally, a longer-term gifting program of the LLC interests to family members, or to trusts for their benefit, may be undertaken. The LLC becomes its own planning currency and allows the management of the collection to be separate from the underlying ownership. Use of the LLC structure may also simplify probate at death, as LLC interests will be transferred, not the art itself. This will avoid the need to retitle the art, change insurance coverage, and the like, since the art will still be owned by the LLC.

Trust Structures

A significant gift of art, or of LLC interests, may be made to a trust using the AEA. Continuing gifts of art, or LLC interests, may be made to the trust using both the annual gift exclusion and taxable gifts above the exemption amount. Over time, a significant amount of art may be transferred for the benefit of the family.

There are several drawbacks to this type of trust, especially during the life of the collector.

First, in addition to the art, the trust will require additional funds to pay the expenses of owning and maintaining art, including insurance.

Second, as mentioned above, the collector must give up possession of the art; otherwise, section 2036 will cause the value of the art to be included in the collector's estate. This requirement to relinquish possession usually ends the discussion. There are some planning techniques, discussed below, that attempt to circumvent the requirement to give up possession.[4]

Third, in addition to the cost of maintaining the art, a trust owning tangible personal property will be more expensive to administer than a trust owning financial assets; in fact, many corporate trustees would refuse to serve as trustee unless this trust were part of a much larger relationship. Either the trustee will need to have expertise in maintaining the collection, or other experts will need to be employed. These same considerations, and others, come into play when a trust such as this is established at death, as discussed in chapter 13.

For these reasons, owning art in a trust is not the same as owning art. The aesthetic, emotional, social, and other experiences of owning art directly are not present when the art is owned by a trust because the art may be locked away somewhere, not on the collector's or trust beneficiaries' walls, and the art cannot be loaned to museums. Furthermore, unless and until the art is either distributed to the beneficiaries or sold and proceeds made available for reinvestment, the beneficiaries are not going to receive any direct or immediate benefits from the trust.

If, after discussing these issues with both advisors and the heirs and finding a suitable trustee, the collector decides to proceed with a trust structure for gifts during life or at death, a number of drafting considerations must be taken into account. Normal trustee powers and duties may need to be altered, especially as they relate to any requirement to invest prudently, diversify investments, and make trust property productive. Trustees will need the right to delegate responsibilities and hire appropriate art experts.[5]

Beyond standard-type trust structures, several types of trusts that are effective for wealth transfer may also be considered when planning with art.

GRATs are irrevocable trusts into which the grantor transfers assets and retains an annuity stream for a period of time, with any assets remaining in the trust at the end of the annuity stream passing to the next generation. GRATs are usually structured so that the present value of the annuity stream is equal to the value of the assets transferred to the GRAT. As a result, any amount remaining in the trust at the expiration of the annuity term passes, in effect, free of both transfer and income taxes to the next generation. As such, GRATs are powerful wealth-transfer planning tools for transferring appreciation on the assets in the GRAT free of any transfer tax. There are a number of variations of GRAT planning and special drafting considerations.

GRATs can be made to work effectively when funded with art but are problematic, since art is fundamentally an illiquid asset. Unless the art is sold, this will require a revaluation of the art each year and a possible transfer of a portion of the art back to the grantor (an in-kind distribution) to pay the annuity, which, in effect, at least partially defeats the purpose of the GRAT in the first place. Funding the GRAT with interests in an Art LLC is more efficient, as it obviates the need to transfer art in and out of the GRAT; rather, LLC units are used as a form of currency for funding the GRAT and paying the annuity if necessary.

A GRAT is a type of GRIT—a grantor-retained interest trust. GRITs used to be popular before antiabuse provisions were enacted as part of the Revenue Reconciliation Act of 1990.[6] Since that time, GRITs may be used only when the remainder gift is to a nonfamily member. A family member includes the donor's spouse, any ancestor or lineal descendant of the donor or the donor's spouse, the donor's siblings, and any spouse of the foregoing. If the collector establishes a GRIT for any such person, the donor's retained interest in the GRIT is deemed to be valued at zero. This means that the entire value of the assets used to fund the GRIT is treated as a taxable gift at the time of funding. Thus, a GRIT will not accomplish any transfer tax planning for a transfer to a family member but only to someone further removed.

So in an instance when a collector wishes to transfer art or other collectibles to a nonfamily member, a GRIT can be useful. Under this technique, the collector transfers art, or LLC interests, to an irrevocable trust, retaining the right to use the art (or any income from the art, or income from the proceeds from the sale of the art) for a certain period of time. When that term expires, ownership of the art (or proceeds if the art is sold) passes to the trust remainderman (or remains in trust for their benefit).

Just as with a GRAT, a gift is made at the time the trust is established. The value of the gift is reduced though, to reflect the value of the interest retained by the collector.

For example, a collector wishes to give his nephew a painting worth $1 million. The collector decides to use a GRIT, transferring the painting to the GRIT but retaining for 10 years the right to use the art and to receive the income from the GRIT if the art is sold. At the end of the 10-year term, the art is either distributed directly to the nephew or retained by the trust for the benefit of the nephew. In either case, the collector no longer has any interest in or right to use the art.

The value of the gift at the time the GRIT is set up and the art contributed to the GRIT is the value of the art, minus the value of the collector's retained interest. To determine this value, we turn to IRC § 7520. Assuming the collector survives the GRIT term, the art and any appreciation are removed from the collector's estate at a gift tax cost that is much less than the estate tax cost would be. The gift tax cost can be lowered still more by extending the term of the GRIT. The gift tax cost will also be affected by the collector's age, with the gift tax cost being reduced inversely to the collector's age.

A variation of the GRIT that some planners have used is sometimes called a TPP-GRIT, which is shorthand for a GRIT that is funded with tangible personal property (which, of course, includes art) but is for family members.

In this scenario, the collector establishes a GRIT for family members, retaining the right to use the art for some term of years. Normally, the gift of the remainder interest is valued as discussed above: by taking the value of the art and subtracting the value of the retained interest using the applicable federal rate under section 7520. However, since we have family members as the remainder beneficiaries, we have to calculate the value of the retained interest without reference to section 7520. Rather, the value of the retained interest must be its actual fair market value or, here, the fair rental value of the art.

To determine fair rental value, it is necessary to obtain an appraisal. The Treasury regulations provide that the best evidence of value is actual rentals that are comparable in nature and character with the property and the duration of the term interest and that without such, little weight would be given to the appraisals.[7]

The challenge is that although there is an active marketplace for rentals of decorative art, there really is not an active marketplace for rentals of museum-quality pieces. And the risk—discussed further below—is that an improper valuation can result in the entire transaction unfolding, with great tax cost as a consequence.

Another popular estate-planning technique for those with taxable estates is known as a sale to an intentionally defective grantor trust (SIDGT). Although there are variations on the theme, the transaction is structured basically as follows. First, an irrevocable trust is formed, which will be a grantor trust for income tax purposes. Although the trust document purposely includes certain powers in favor of the grantor, the trustee, or even the beneficiary, the trust is referred to as "defective." What this means is that the trust does not exist for federal income tax purposes even though it is a valid trust for all other purposes. All income tax consequences inside the trust automatically flow out to the grantor.

Then art or, more likely, interests in an LLC owning art are sold (rather than gifted) by the grantor to the trust, usually for a long-term promissory note. Normally when someone sells something, any gain realized is required to be recognized. However, because the trust is "defective" as to the seller, since the trust and the seller are one and the same for federal income tax purposes, no gain is recognized.

The art, either directly or beneficially through the LLC, is now owned by the IDGT, not the collector. That effectively freezes the value for the collector at the face amount of the note. Any further appreciation in the art above the interest rate that is charged is owned by, and accrues to the benefit of, the IDGT and its beneficiaries.

The note itself may take one of three forms: an installment note, with very low interest rates currently; a self-canceling installment note; or a private annuity. Each of these structures has benefits and detriments, depending on the age and the health of the collector. Each carries an interest component, and appreciation above this interest component escapes transfer taxation in the collector's estate.

The main challenges with all of these advanced planning techniques, such as the GRAT, GRIT, and SIDGT (and a variation of the SIDGT, a beneficiary defective inheritor's trust [BDIT]), are, first, liquidity; second, valuation; and perhaps the greatest of all, the requirement to relinquish possession of the art.

To address these problems, some advisors have taken the following approach. First, the collector contributes the art to an LLC. The collector then establishes an IDGT and funds the trust with cash or other assets, typically at least 10 percent of the value of the art. Next, the collector sells LLC interests to the IDGT, and since the trust is a grantor trust, no capital gain is recognized. The sale is made for some cash, perhaps the amount originally funded to the trust, but mostly for a note from the IDGT to the collector.

This is a fairly common wealth-transfer technique for high-net-worth families with other types of assets. This technique has been especially popular in the recent past because of low interest rates under section 7520. For a transaction completed in December 2018, the note could carry an interest rate as low as 2.68 percent for a note with a maturity of up to nine years or 3.0 percent for a longer-term note. The note may also be interest-only for some period of time and then use some amortization period but with the majority of the note being due as a balloon payment. Again, there are many variations on a theme in this type of transaction. All earnings and appreciation above that interest rate pass to the next generation(s) transfer tax free.

Cash to pay the principal and interest on the note will come from the LLC, most of which is owned by the IDGT. The LLC in turn will receive cash from leasing the art back to the collector. This rent will be paid pursuant to a lease agreement that sets the rental at a market rate, as determined by appraisal.

On paper, and assuming that all documentation and appraisals are done in a professional manner, this transaction should work effectively. But this transaction is not without significant risks—namely, (1) availability of discounting at the time of sale of LLC interests to IDGT, (2) determination of the fair rental value in the absence of an active rental market of high-end art, and (3) section 2036 issues, since the collector may at all times retain physical possession of the art.

The key component to this transaction is the fair rental value appraisal. I am aware of a number of highly qualified appraisal firms that are comfortable preparing such an appraisal; I am also aware of a number of highly qualified appraisal firms that are not comfortable preparing this type of appraisal. Certainly, in theory, this is a valid technique; however, it does carry the risks outlined above, especially given the fact that any such appraisal is based on market rental rates from an essentially nonexistent market.

Early in 2017, an IRS audit was settled that involved this issue. In that case, which is not reported since it was settled, corporate-owned artwork was displayed in the home of one of the principal owners of the corporation. Under federal income tax law, this was deemed to be a distribution of property from the corporation to one of its shareholders, better known as a dividend. And what was the amount of the dividend? The fair rental value of the artwork! Perhaps fortunately for the taxpayer, but not so fortunately for the art planning community, the case was settled and does not provide any precedential value to others regarding the validity of determining fair rental value or the appropriate valuation method.

This is why it is imperative to know the collector's goals. Do they want to keep the collection intact and transfer it to their family, or are they trying to accomplish significant wealth transfer by using an illiquid asset rather than parting with liquidity?

Whatever is done, Form 709, Federal Gift Tax Return, should be filed even if no gift tax is due. The filing of a gift tax return starts the statute of limitations on the value of the transferred art.

And, most important, if you make a gift, you must deliver the property. Retaining physical possession of the art undercuts any planning that you do even if you have otherwise documented the transaction.

Summary

Giving the art to family members during life may be the right choice. But if the goal is wealth transfer, which is different from planning with art, then a collector should consider accomplishing that wealth transfer with different assets. Because of the limitations on discounting art, it is perhaps the most expensive asset to give away during life.

Notes

1. I am assuming that the reader has a basic understanding of the transfer tax system, and I do not cite to the relevant IRC sections for that reason. Estate taxes are addressed in IRC §§ 2001 *et seq.*; gift taxes are addressed in IRC §§ 2501 *et seq.*; generation-skipping transfer taxes are addressed in IRC §§ 2601 *et seq.*

2. Stone v. United States, No. CV-06-00259-TEH, 2007 U.S. Dist. LEXIS 38332 (N.D. Cal. May 25, 2007), *aff'd sub nom.* Stone Trust Agreement v. United States, 2009 U.S. App. LEXIS 6349 (9th Cir. Mar. 24, 2009).

3. Estate of Elkins v. Comm'r, 140 T.C. 86 (Mar. 11, 2013). For an excellent discussion of both the Tax Court and Court of Appeals decisions, see Jeff Baskies, *Discounts Permitted for Fractional Interests in Artwork: The Fascinating 5th Circuit Opinion in Estate of James A. Elkins, Jr. v. Commissioner*, STEVE LEIMBERG'S EST. PLAN. NEWSL., no. 2247, Sept. 25, 2014.

4. IRC § 2036.

5. For more on trust drafting considerations, see the excellent discussion in Michael Duffy, *Whom Do You Trust with Your Picasso? Planning Considerations for Trusts That Hold Title to Works of Art*, PROB. & PROP., Sept./Oct. 2013.

6. Pub. L. No. 101-508, enacted Nov. 5, 1990, applicable to transfers after Oct. 8, 1990.

7. See discussion in chapter 4 regarding appraisals.

11

Donating—During Life

We have already seen that selling during life and gifting during life are expensive options. They may be the right options for individual pieces or for the collection as a whole, but they are expensive from both a tax and a nontax point of view. Selling involves both tax and transactional costs; gifting involves both tax and wealth-transfer opportunity costs. So for those who desire to keep their collection intact, the "charitable solution" may be the best option.

Donating artwork to museums (and other charities) is a well-established option, with most major art museums in the United States, perhaps in the world as well, having been started by one person or family. The Kimbell, Amon Carter, and Sid Richardson art museums in Fort Worth, Texas; the Philbrook and the Gilcrease art museums in Tulsa, Oklahoma; and, most recently, Crystal Bridges in Bentonville, Arkansas, are just a few examples close to the author's home—world-class museums that were started from one person's passion and collection.

In addition to the tax benefits of donating art to charity, the collector may feel great personal satisfaction from sharing privately held art with the general public. But donating art to a museum is much more complicated than one might think, from both a tax and a nontax point of view.

Donating art to charity is subject to all of the federal income tax rules applicable to charitable giving generally and to several special rules applicable to charitable donations of art specifically. Beyond the federal income, gift, and estate tax charitable deduction rules, the collector must always remember to comply with appraisal and substantiation requirements.

The amount of the federal income tax charitable deduction available to a taxpayer is primarily dependent on (1) the type of asset contributed and (2) the type of charitable recipient to which it is contributed.

For federal income tax charitable deduction purposes, there are essentially four types of assets: cash, ordinary income property, long-term capital gain property, and tangible personal property unrelated to the mission of the charity. Some people break some of these asset categories down further, but we are going to focus on just two categories, so further breakdown is not necessary for our purposes.

For federal income tax charitable deduction purposes, there are essentially two types of charities: public charities, sometimes referred to as "50 percent charities," and private charities, sometimes referred to as "30 percent charities." Again, some people further break down these categories, but that is not necessary for our analysis. We will take a closer look at one of those types of charities below when discussing "Your Own Museum."

Combining the type of asset contributed with the type of charity to which it is donated determines the amount of the federal income tax charitable deduction.

- If you give cash to a public charity, you may deduct 100 percent of the amount of cash, up to 50 percent of your adjusted gross income (AGI). This was modified by the 2017 Tax Act, in that the AGI limit was increased to 60 percent if all contributions during the tax year are made in cash.
- If you give cash to a private charity, you may deduct 100 percent of the amount of cash, up to 30 percent of your AGI.
- If you give ordinary income property to a public charity, you may deduct the lesser of the fair market value or your cost basis in the ordinary income property, up to 50 percent of your AGI.
- If you give ordinary income property to a private charity, you may deduct the lesser of the fair market value or your cost basis in the ordinary income property, up to 20 percent of your AGI.
- If you give long-term capital gain property to a public charity, you may deduct its fair market value, up to 30 percent of your AGI.

- If you give long-term capital gain property to a private charity, you may deduct its fair market value, up to 20 percent of your AGI, if it is publicly traded stock; otherwise, your income tax charitable deduction is limited to your cost basis.
- If you give tangible personal property unrelated to the charity's purpose to a public charity, you may deduct the lesser of its fair market value or your cost basis, up to 50 percent of your AGI.
- If you give tangible personal property unrelated to the charity's purpose to a private charity, you may deduct the lesser of its fair market value or your cost basis, up to 20 percent of your AGI.

Any amount donated in a particular tax year that is in excess of the AGI limitation may be carried forward and deducted, subject to the same annual AGI limitations, for up to five years.

Whew!

Let's narrow that down to art and to donations made by collectors. Charitable donations by artists are subject to the second category above—that is, donations of ordinary income property—and are further discussed in chapter 17.

For collectors and investors, art is a capital asset. The federal income tax treatment of the donation of art depends on (1) how long the art has been owned by the collector, (2) the type of charitable recipient, and (3) how the charitable recipient intends to use the art.

Let's assume the collector has owned the art to be donated for over one year. Ownership for a lesser time would mean that it is short-term capital gain property, which makes it less attractive (from a federal income tax charitable deduction point of view) ordinary income property, as it would give rise to a cost-basis deduction to the donor as opposed to its assumed higher fair market value. So rule #1 is to make sure you have owned the art for more than one year.

A donation of long-term capital gain property (the third category above) entitles the donor to a federal income tax charitable deduction equal to the fair market value of the property, capped at 30 percent of the donor's AGI if given to a public charity (including a private operating foundation, discussed below) or 20 percent of the donor's AGI if given to a private charity. Since this is art and not publicly traded stock, a further limit applies in this case; that is, the federal income tax charitable deduction for a donation of art to a private charity is limited to cost basis as opposed to the again assumed higher fair market value. So rule #2 is to make the donation to a public charity.

So far, subject to the rules discussed below, if you donate art to a public charity (or private operating foundation), such as a museum, then you may deduct for federal income tax purposes an amount equal to its fair market value, capped at 30 percent of your AGI. If you made that same gift to your own (nonoperating) private foundation, your federal income tax charitable deduction would be limited to your cost basis rather than fair market value and to 20 percent of your AGI. In either case, excess deductions can be carried forward for five years.

But there are other rules. In tax planning in general and in the federal income tax charitable deduction arena in particular, certain perceived taxpayer abuses have led to more and more anti-tax-abuse rules. Three of those rules—the related-use rule, the partial interest rule, and the fractional interest rule—are discussed below.

Related-Use Rule

Art is tangible personal property (the fourth category above), and donations of tangible personal property are treated differently, depending on how they are intended to be used by the recipient charity. If the intended use of the art by the recipient charity is deemed "related" to the charity's tax-exempt purposes, then the donor will be entitled to a federal income tax charitable deduction at its fair market value (subject to the 30 percent AGI cap); if the use is "unrelated" to the recipient charity's tax-exempt purpose, then the donor's federal income tax charitable deduction will be limited to cost basis in the art (though up to 50 percent of the donor's AGI). This assumes that the collector has owned the art for more than a year before the donation and that the charity is a public charity (or private operating foundation).

What is a related use? Clearly, if a painting is contributed to an art museum and the art museum states its intention to add the painting to its permanent collection, then it is a related use. Likewise, a painting contributed to a university to be used for educational purposes, being placed in its library for viewing and study by art students, would qualify as a related use. If the school (or any other charity for that matter), however, intended and in fact sold the painting and added the proceeds to its endowment, that is not a related use, and the donor would be limited to a cost-basis deduction.[1]

Compliance with the related-use rule was revised by the Pension Protection Act of 2006, which expanded the requirements in IRC § 170. It added a new section 170(e)(7)(A), which effectively restricts the donor's federal income tax charitable deduction to cost basis if the charity sells the property within three years of receipt unless the charity provides a certification that the property was put to a related use or at least was intended to be put to a related use at the time of donation. This does not mean that the art absolutely cannot be sold by the charity within three years; it means that, absent the required certification from the charity, any sale within three years from the donation will limit the donor's federal income tax charitable deduction to cost basis.

This is both a substantive rule and a compliance rule. The substantive rule is that the charity must certify its intended use at the time of the donation. The compliance rule is that if the charity does in fact sell the tangible personal property within the three-year time period, it must file an amended Form 8282, reflecting the actual sales price. If the actual sales price is substantially different from the originally claimed federal income tax charitable deduction, that could trigger an audit of the original deduction.

Some charities are willing to accept donations with the proviso that they will not sell the work for three years. This is not compliance with the substantive part of the rule; it is a way to avoid the requirement that an amended filing be made. Technically, if the IRS were to learn that a piece was sold after the three-year period and the charity did not originally comply with the substantive requirement that the original donation be intended for use to further the charity's tax-exempt purpose at the time of donation, the original deduction could be limited to cost basis. Therefore, it is imperative that the collector donor obtain from the charitable recipient its statement of its bona fide intended use at the time of donation.

As a result of these rules, a donation of art should be made only to a public charity or private operating foundation (see "Your Own Museum," below) and only to a charity that will satisfy the related-use rule. Practically speaking, that means donating to an art museum or other public charity that will use the art as part of its mission. As mentioned above, a related use specifically does not include the charity selling the art and adding the proceeds to its endowment.

To satisfy this rule, I encourage clients to obtain from the recipient charity a letter specifically stating its intended use of the art. It is possible that the use may change—the museum or other charity may subsequently determine to sell the work. What matters is the legitimate, intended use of the artwork at the time of donation. This related-use letter is in addition to other required substantiation, including an appraisal and Form 8382.[2]

Partial Interest Rule

The partial interest rule applies to any donation to charity when a donor makes a gift but retains a "substantial interest" in the property donated to charity. Simply stated, a donation of a partial interest in any type of property will not entitle the donor to a federal income tax charitable deduction.[3] There are exceptions to this rule, some of which will be discussed below.

This is particularly important in the world of art. Most often, a purchaser of art acquires the art only—and not the copyright to the art. However, if the collector were to own both the piece of art and the copyright, then any donation must include both the art and the copyright for the donor to be entitled to a federal income tax charitable deduction. If the collector donated the art but retained the copyright, or vice versa, no federal income tax charitable deduction would be available.

Special rules apply to artists and are discussed below in chapters 17 through 19.

A growing trend in the art world is "affinity marketing." Some artists and galleries are following a practice much like that of TOM's Shoes, which gives away a pair of shoes to a person in need for every pair of shoes that consumers buy, or of Starbucks, which gives away a percentage of its sales to charities of its choice. But this gives rise to some special federal income tax charitable deduction issues as well.

Case Study

A collector desired to buy a particular painting from a particular artist. To even be allowed to enter the bidding process, the collector had to agree that if they successfully purchased the painting, they would donate the painting to a museum within a stated number of years after the acquisition. All of this had to be in writing, up front, with the museum designated, and further, the museum would have to agree now that it would accept the painting when donated.

Several issues were apparent to me. First, is this a partial interest, which would mean no deduction for the collector when they made the donation? Was this a purchase of a term of years, which would mean that the painting had no value or at least a reduced value at the time of donation, thereby impacting the charitable deduction? And would the museum agree to certify when the donation was actually made that it would satisfy the requirements of the related-use rule in the future?

The staff at the gallery selling the art were a bit surprised; in fact, they said that they had been doing this for years and nobody had raised these issues before!

Why would the gallery impose this requirement? An artist's work achieves its highest value when it has been displayed in one or more museums. This has not only the intangible benefit of enhancing the artist's reputation but also the commercial benefit of increasing the value and price of other works by the artist. Hence, a form of affinity marketing.

In this particular case, all of these issues were addressed to the satisfaction of the gallery, the collector, and the museum. The museum, by the way, is a world-class, well-known museum, which accepted this type of donation for the first time in its history!

Case Study

In a similar situation, an artist would agree to sell one of his works to a collector only if the collector would agree to donate the work to a museum either during life or at death. This again raised the issues of whether this might be a partial interest (probably not) or a purchase of a life estate or term of years, which would significantly decrease the value of the federal income tax or estate tax charitable deduction, perhaps to zero!

From the artist's point of view, this requirement would enhance his legacy, which is perfectly understandable.

Only time will tell if the proffered solution will work. The collector offered to buy the work, but instead of entering into a contractual obligation to donate the work to a museum at death (or earlier), the collector would make a charitable pledge of the artwork. Whether a charitable pledge is enforceable is a matter of state law, and if the pledge is made in a state where such pledges are not enforceable, then perhaps the collector will be able to maintain the ability to take a federal income tax charitable deduction if the donation is completed during life or a federal estate tax charitable deduction if the donation is made by bequest.

As mentioned earlier, donating art is not as easy as it looks!

Fractional Interest Rule

A long-standing technique, though perhaps used less today than in the past, is a donation of a fractional interest in a painting.

First off, it is important that it is a fractional interest, not a partial interest. Let's say that you own a painting worth $120,000, plus you own the copyright to the painting (as pointed out above, that is unusual for a collector). A permissible fractional interest charitable donation would arise if you donated a 10 percent undivided fractional interest in the painting and 10 percent of the copyright to a museum. An impermissible partial interest charitable donation would arise if you donated some percentage of the painting but kept all of the copyright. As pointed out above, if the donor keeps a "substantial interest" in the painting—the copyright—the value of the partial interest that is donated—the painting—is not deductible at all. Donations of fractional interests, on the other hand, are deductible, assuming all of the other rules applicable to charitable donations of art are satisfied.

So partial interests are out, but fractional interest giving has been quite popular over the years.

Here's how it used to work. Say you have the same $120,000 painting (but no interest in the copyright, which is usually retained by the artist).

One year you decide you need a $10,000 federal income tax charitable deduction, so you give the community art museum near your summer home a 1/12 fractional interest in the painting. The museum might or might not take possession of the painting for its share of the time. In the past, you were entitled to a 1/12, or $10,000, federal income tax charitable deduction. Notice that you were not "penalized" by having to take a fractional interest discount.

Time passes. A few years later you discover that your painting has appreciated and is now valued at $240,000. And you decide that this year, you need a $20,000 federal income tax charitable deduction. So you donate another 1/12 of the painting, now valued at $20,000. That little museum near your summer home? It still has not decided if it wants to bother with showing the painting two months out of the year even though it is legally entitled to.

You guessed it . . . more time passes, and more appreciation happens. And now you want more and more federal income tax charitable deduction for giving away successive fractional interests in the same painting, which, by the way, still hangs in the same frame, on the same hook, in the same room, over the same couch, in your same house, after all of these years.

Believe it or not, that was fairly standard practice, at least until the passage of the Pension Protection Act of 2006 and the introduction of the fractional interest rule, version 1.1. That's my terminology, by the way—not the terminology of Congress or the IRS.

That rule said, yes, you can do fractional interest donations to charity, but several conditions must be met. First, you must complete a donation of the entire interest in the work of art by the earlier of 10 years from the date of the first fractional interest gift or your death. That caused collectors to become much more concerned about their life expectancies! It also caused younger donors to rethink this strategy.

Second, you may donate successive fractional interests, but the value that you use to calculate the federal income tax charitable deduction for the first fractional gift is the value you must use for all successive fractional interest gifts. Referring back to the above example, all successive gifts would be valued at their percentage of the original $120,000 value, regardless of appreciation and regardless of the actual value of the painting at the time of the successive fractional gifts.

Third, the organization had to take actual possession of the art for its ownership period.

Version 1.1 of the fractional interest rule was overkill. It intended to do away with a perceived federal income tax abuse of using successively higher values for successive fractional gifts while still keeping the painting right there in the family room. But it went too far and negatively impacted perfectly legitimate fractional donations. Let's say gift #1 was at the $120,000 value but gift #2 was made at a time when the painting was valued at $240,000. Subsequent fractional gifts would be limited to the original value for federal income tax charitable deduction purposes but would result in a taxable gift because the value of the charitable gift tax deduction was also frozen by version 1.1. The same was true if the collector died before transferring the entire value, as the estate tax deduction value was also frozen at the original value. That was not the intent of the fractional interest rule, which was enacted to prevent a perceived income tax abuse. Once again, the law of unintended consequences struck and brought the practice of fractional interest donations to a halt.

Fortunately, version 1.2, or 2.1, came along and clarified that the valuation freeze applies only to the federal income tax charitable deduction, not for federal estate or gift tax charitable deduction purposes.

Finally, we look at some practical points about fractional interest gifts. It is unlikely that a museum will accept a fractional interest in artwork without at least the expectation that it will eventually own the entire work. This may just be expected, or it may actually be a condition of accepting the first fractional gift. Second, physical possession should change hands, and depending on the size and condition of the artwork, its packaging, transportation, and insurance should be agreed upon in advance. A joint-ownership agreement of sorts should be entered into and agreement reached on allocation of expenses. Finally, a periodic appraisal should be performed, for nontax reasons as well as tax reasons, as discussed in the chapter 4 on valuation.

Putting This into Practice

With those rules, and the reasons for them, in mind, let's examine how one may make donations of art or otherwise make art available for others in the context of charitable giving.

The simplest approach is a direct donation of the art to an art museum or other qualifying charitable organization, keeping in mind the related-use rule. The collector will be entitled to a federal income tax charitable deduction equal to the full fair market value of the donated art, up to 30 percent of AGI, with a carryforward of any excess for up to five tax years.

Although perhaps not as common as in the past, a donation of a fractional interest in art is still feasible as long as the collector understands and complies with the fractional interest rules. If it is a piece that the collector intends to leave to the museum eventually, it may make sense for the collector to make a donation of a fraction and loan the remainder of the piece to the museum. This avoids the problem of moving the piece back and forth, where damage is most likely to occur. The collector may then make further donations of fractional interests, timed to most efficiently utilize the federal income tax charitable deduction.

Another option with respect to moving art back and forth is to think outside the box or, in this case, the calendar year. Rather than moving the art to and from the charity each calendar year, the collector and the charity can enter into a multiyear loan agreement so that each maintains possession for its respective ownership period but over a longer period of time—say, three or five years—so that the piece does not have to be moved as frequently.

The *Elkins* case, discussed in chapter 10, suggests that a valuation discount is permissible for fractional interests of art transferred to family members. Until now, no such discount has been required for fractional interest donations of art to museums or other charities. It is unclear what, if any, effect *Elkins* will have on this practice, and readers are advised to consult with their tax counsel before making fractional interest gifts to charity.

This all sounds simple, but it is anything but. Most art museums have much more art in their existing inventory than they will display in a lifetime. And as more and more collectors seek a museum home for their collections, they are finding it increasingly difficult to identify a museum willing to accept their art. Some collectors are turning to educational institutions or health-care facilities, where the use of the art will satisfy the related-use rule, while others are establishing their own museums. However, collectors should not take for granted that museums or other acceptable charities will accept their work. This is especially so when leaving art to museums or other charities at death, as discussed in chapter 14.

Do not be surprised if you are asked to contribute some amount of liquid assets to support your donation. Maintaining art is expensive, and it is understandable that the museum might ask for contributions to help cover the future costs of storage, insurance, and curation of your art.

Be prepared to discuss the terms of your donation. Will your art be part of the museum's permanent collection? Can it be loaned to other museums and exhibits? Must it be displayed a certain amount of time? What are naming opportunities? These conversations should be held early in the process, both for lifetime giving and for donations that will take place at death. A recent article discusses considerations that should be taken into account when discussing possible donation with a museum.[4]

Case Study

A collector couple donated several valuable pieces of sculpture to a regional museum near their summer home, in anticipation that it would not only become part of the permanent collection (it has) but also be displayed at least periodically. That was almost a decade ago, and the pieces are still in storage and have never been displayed.

The collectors are now considering donating several more significant pieces of art in the same geographic area, but given past experience, these pieces will not be donated to the same museum. They have been encouraged to have conversations with the executive directors and curatorial staff of several different museums that may be better positioned to help them achieve their goal of sharing their art with the public.

What about loans? Lending artwork to a museum or to a tour among museums is quite common and allows many people who would not otherwise have the opportunity to view the artwork to see it on display. But there are absolutely no federal income tax consequences for anyone involved. A loan of artwork to charity will not generate a federal income tax charitable deduction and will not be considered a charitable donation.[5] On a positive note, this means the collector will not need to obtain an appraisal of the art. However, collectors contemplating loans of artwork should consult with their advisors and enter into a loan agreement with the museum that addresses all of the issues discussed herein, including term of the loan, risk-management responsibilities, shipping, storage, and other terms. Finally, collectors should not loan art to a private nonoperating foundation, as such a transfer will be considered to be a taxable gift.

Case Study

A collector recently asked me whether a loan of artwork to a museum could be considered a charitable gift, valued at its fair rental value! Interesting question, but unfortunately, there is no legal authority for this position.

Charitable remainder trusts (CRTs) are popular income tax planning tools. Basically, a CRT is an irrevocable trust, into which you place appreciated assets, the assets are sold, and no federal income or capital gain taxes are currently due because the CRT is a tax-exempt entity. As most commonly structured, the CRT will pay an income stream back to the donor (and spouse) for life, with the remainder then passing to charity. The donor is entitled to a federal income tax charitable deduction equal to the present value of the remainder interest (again, subject to all of the limits that apply to charitable gifts), and the donor is able to diversify a low-basis, highly appreciated asset without currently paying federal income or capital gains tax. A full description of CRTs is beyond the scope of this book, but that is the basic structure, and it suffices for our purposes.

Although the planner must always consider whether a CRT works well in a particular situation, CRTs do not work particularly well with art—or with any other type of tangible personal property for that matter. First, a federal income tax charitable deduction is not available until the art or other collectible is actually sold by the CRT trustee.[6] Second, the gift will always fail the related-use test, so the deduction, when available, will be limited to the lesser of fair market value or cost basis, presumably the latter.[7] Finally, CRTs must allow the trustee to reinvest the trust principal into productive assets. This means that a CRT formed with the intention of holding art, rather than selling art and reinvesting the proceeds, will probably not even qualify as a CRT, meaning the trust will not be exempt from federal income tax. All of this is not to say that there are not times when a CRT might work, but they will be few and far between.

Case Study

I was recently asked if it might not be possible to achieve a fair market value federal income tax deduction using a CRT funded with art. The theory is that since no federal income tax charitable deduction is available until the tangible personal property is sold and at that time the asset held by the CRT is cash, not tangible personal property, the rules pertaining to a donation of cash should apply, thereby avoiding the imposition of the related-use rule. Again, an interesting theory, but there is no legal authority to support this position.

If the planner and collector determine that a CRT does in fact make sense in their particular planning case, then it is usually advisable to use a particular type of CRT known as a FLIP-CRUT. This type of CRT starts off as a net income charitable remainder unitrust (NICRUT or NIMCRUT)—meaning it pays out the lesser of a stated percentage of trust principal or actual trust income—until the art is sold; then it "flips" to become a standard charitable remainder unitrust (SCRUT or STANCRUT), meaning it pays out a stated percentage of whatever the trust's principal balance actually is determined to be each year.

Putting these rules and practicalities together, the use of a CRT is generally limited to the situation where the collector plans to sell the art within the first year of the CRT and is content to receive a limited, and delayed, federal income tax charitable deduction.

Bargain sales are a part sale, part gift to charity and are effective for estate planning with art. A bargain sale is simply a sale of the artwork to a charity at a price less than the fair market value. The difference in value is a charitable gift, eligible for a federal income tax charitable deduction, subject to all of the other limitations that apply to charitable gifts. The collector must allocate cost basis between the charitable and noncharitable parts of the transaction, and any gain attributable to the sale part of the transaction must be recognized by the collector. However, depending on the actual terms of the bargain sale, the federal income tax charitable deduction may offset the gain realized on the sale of the noncharitable portion of the transaction.

For example, a collector has a painting worth about $14 million, about $6 million in other liquid assets, and two adult daughters. The collector wants the painting to stay in the family (although she had not asked the Big Question: How do the daughters feel about the painting?). Federal estate taxes on this estate, under 2018 laws, would be approximately $3.52 million, leaving a $14 million painting and $2.48 million in liquid assets before paying any other expenses.

Theoretically, the simplest solution would be for each daughter to receive a 50 percent undivided interest in the painting and 50 percent of the remaining liquid assets. But is this really so simple? Where does the painting hang? If each daughter wants it half the time, even if only to make sure the other does not get it all of the time, this very valuable painting will have to be moved periodically. Packaging and shipping are expensive, and that is when the art is most exposed to damage. And what if one or both of the daughters do not have suitable quarters in which to display and maintain the painting?

What if one daughter wants to sell, but the other does not? There is no real market for fractional interests in artwork, so it is not realistic to think that less than the entire work could be sold. This could lead to an expensive partition action.

To avoid these issues, the collector should, first, have a conversation with the daughters to see if they have any real interest in the painting—not the value of the painting but the painting itself—or if they would be content to visit it periodically in a museum, perhaps in an area of the museum that in some fashion recognizes the family for the contribution of the painting.

Assuming that neither daughter has a passion to possess the painting (or the means to be able to house such a piece—remember, security, fire and smoke, etc.), it might be possible, depending on cash flow needs, to work with a local museum that has acquisition funds available (not all museums do) to negotiate a part sale, part gift transfer to the museum.

By way of example, assume that the painting is worth $14 million, that it has a basis of $1 million (from prior estate step-up), and that the mother has a combined federal and state income tax rate of 40 percent and a combined long-term capital gain rate of 33 percent (remember, collectibles are taxed at 28 percent for federal purposes). A bargain sale takes place for $7 million, exactly 50 percent of the value. One-half of the basis is allocated to the noncharitable share, so that the mother recognizes $6.5 million of gain. She also has $500,000 of other ordinary income.

Much of the gain, however, is offset by the charitable deduction. Her entire income would have been offset by the federal income tax charitable deduction except that the current year deduction is limited to 30 percent of AGI. Oversimplifying, 30 percent of her income of $7 million, or $2.1 million, is currently deductible, with the balance of $4.9 million being carried forward to offset income in the next five years (limited to 30 percent of AGI each year).

From the $7 million in cash received from the sale, approximately $1,650,000 is used to pay income taxes, so she is able to add $5,350,000 to her investment account. She has $4.9 million of charitable deduction carryforward, which could be worth approximately $1,960,000 in federal income tax savings if fully utilized. If there is a risk of not using the entire charitable deduction carryforward, the bargain sale could actually be stretched over several years and combined with fractional interest giving to lengthen the time available for the carryforward. This would be accomplished, perhaps, by entering into a bargain sale for 50 percent of the painting in the current year and then doing the balance of the bargain sale in the future, after the charitable deduction carryforward from the initial sale is completely utilized. The fractional interest rules must also be complied with in a scenario such as this.

Perhaps most important, the painting will be housed in a local museum, which will give appropriate recognition to the gift, and she (and her daughters) can view the painting as much as they like. They are no longer responsible for its upkeep and insurance.

Whether this type of planning works is fact dependent, but it is worth considering in the right circumstances.

Charitable lead trusts (CLTs) are powerful federal income, estate, and gift tax planning tools. A CLT is an irrevocable trust that, in its most common form, pays an income stream to charity for a period of time (which may be tied to the donor's lifetime), with the remainder of the trust coming back into the family. As with CRTs, there are many variations on a theme with CLT planning. A basic planning point is that the CLT has to be either a grantor trust—which entitles the donor to an immediate federal income tax charitable deduction equal to the present value of the payments going to charity but then requires the donor to pay taxes on all income earned by the trust—or a nongrantor trust—whereby the donor forgoes the federal income tax charitable deduction in favor of the powerful wealth-transfer characteristics of this type of CLT.

CLTs can be set up during life or at death. When planning with art, CLTs are more commonly used in the latter case, with the CLT being established by the donor's will. This is because the CLT, unlike a CRT, is not an income-tax-exempt entity, meaning that either the grantor or the CLT itself will incur federal income taxes. This is discussed in chapter 14.

A charitable gift annuity (CGA) might also work in limited circumstances. A CGA is a contract with a charity, whereby the donor contributes assets to the charity in return for a promise to pay an annuity to the donor for his or her lifetime or for joint lives with a spouse. The difference in amount between the present value of the annuity and the total amount of the gift is a charitable gift, deductible in accordance with the rules that apply to charitable gifts generally.

For federal income tax purposes, the collector will recognize a capital gain, spread over the life of the annuity, of the difference between the cost basis and the fair market value of the art. Basis is allocated in the same manner as for a bargain sale.

The biggest drawback to a CGA is that not all charities can offer CGAs. In fact, CGAs are most often offered by educational and medical institutions that have large constituencies. Therefore, it is unlikely that a museum or other appropriate recipient of a donation of artwork would qualify to issue CGAs.

However, where a museum is able to partner with another charity, such as a community foundation, to offer a CGA, a transfer to a museum could be arranged that would be similar to the bargain sale scenario discussed above but would use a CGA. The biggest obstacles are the charity's ability to issue the CGA and the donor's status as an unsecured creditor of the charity involved. Again, different facts lead to different solutions, and planners should not automatically close the door on any possible solution.

Your Own Museum

As mentioned above, many of the major art museums in this country, and perhaps the world, started with one person's or one family's art collection. For a client with a truly significant collection, the formation of their own museum may be an appropriate solution. Both tax and nontax factors must be considered.

Case Study

A successful entrepreneur had over the years built a significant and unique art collection now valued at over $400 million. The collector's family was financially secure from other investments and previous wealth-transfer planning. The collector wanted her collection to remain intact. She was aware of other museums started by collectors to preserve their collections. Having been in the real estate business, she already owned several properties that she felt could be converted to a museum space.

In the course of planning, the collector was made aware of the significant costs involved in operating a museum. Although she already had a building that could be used, she was made aware of remodeling costs, staffing requirements and costs, and endowment needs to maintain the collection and facility in perpetuity. After reviewing all of the costs involved, the collector decided that a better course of action was to work with an existing museum with compatible art. As a result, the collector is paying to renovate an existing area of the museum, which will henceforth be dedicated in her name, to show her collection.

For a number of reasons, a collector may not wish to transfer his or her collection to an existing museum, either during life or at death. Perhaps the collector cannot find a museum suitable for the collection, or the collector is not comfortable with the conditions imposed by any suitable museum for accepting their collection.

Still, because of the significant costs of establishing and maintaining a museum, collectors should first seek out existing museums that satisfy their requirements in terms of space, location, infrastructure, and shared aesthetic interests. This may be preferable even if it means paying to build a separate wing onto an existing facility to house and guarantee the integrity of the collection.

Case Study

A collector had built a substantial collection of impressionistic art, valued in the range of $200 million. This was certainly of a size to justify creating a museum; still, after reviewing the costs of doing so, the collector agreed to first explore working with an existing museum.

One of the collector's conditions was that the collection be displayed permanently and in its entirety. The collection was not to go off of display and was not to be loaned to other institutions or go on tour. One may not agree with that view, but it is important to remember that collectors are free to set whatever conditions they wish (as long as they do not jeopardize the federal income tax charitable deduction or otherwise violate rules governing the operation of private foundations).

The problem here was that no museum would agree to these conditions in perpetuity, even if given a sizable endowment to support the collection, and no reasonable accommodation could be found. Therefore, this collector determined that the only acceptable course of action was to build a museum and fund an endowment to support its operations.

Not everyone has the means to establish a museum, and collectors should always first explore the costs of establishing and operating a museum, which may encourage them to seek out other solutions. If no other alternatives are available, then the collector may wish to form his or her own museum. If the collector wishes to establish the museum as a tax-exempt organization and to receive a federal income tax charitable deduction for contributions to the museum, then the museum will be formed as a private operating foundation (POF). It will be considered a "private foundation" because it is being funded by one person or family and will not meet the tests required to qualify for public charity status through either its activities or its sources of support. It will be considered "operating" because it will actually conduct its own tax-exempt charitable activities, not just make grants to other operating charities in the manner of a private nonoperating foundation.

As such, a POF is a hybrid entity, but because it is operating a charitable activity, it will be treated much like a public charity, as discussed above. The donor will be entitled to a federal income tax charitable deduction of up to 50 percent of their AGI for cash contributions to the POF rather than 30 percent of their AGI for cash contributions to a nonoperating private foundation. Perhaps more significantly, the donor/creator will be entitled to a federal income tax charitable deduction equal to the fair market value of the collection that is given to the POF, subject to the 30 percent AGI limit in any one year. This will tend to be a large donation, so it may make sense to work with the team of advisors to determine how and when to actually contribute the collection. It is likely that if the collector creates the POF during life, the collection will be contributed over time to stagger the deduction and to more efficiently use it against income of the collector. It is possible that some works will be contributed and others loaned for a period of time or that fractional interest gifts will be made to arrive at the most income-tax-efficient solution.

The collector, as creator of the POF, may also act as its president and, within reason, maintain a high degree of control over the collection.

A POF must meet its own special set of rules to qualify as such. Although highly technical, the rules in actuality are not difficult to meet for someone who wishes to organize and operate a legitimate museum. In fact, many museums are POFs, as they have been created by a single donor or a single family. Sometimes they remain as POFs in perpetuity; other times they are able to convert to public charity status after raising the required percentage of operating funds from other donors. This decision to become a public charity is largely a matter of "optics," as it is more difficult for POFs to raise money from the public for operations than it is for public charities to do so.

POFs must meet several tests.[8] All POFs must meet an income test, as well as an asset test or an endowment test or a support test.

The income test means that the POF spends substantially all of the lesser of its adjusted net income or its minimum investment return (5 percent of its investment assets) directly for the active conduct of its charitable purpose. This includes any money spent to acquire or maintain the art and any necessary administration expenses. This test is easily passed by any legitimate museum operation.[9]

can't support either you or the POF

In addition to the income test, all POFs must pass one of three alternative tests: the asset test, the endowment test, or the support test.

The asset test basically requires that substantially more than half of the POF's assets (65 percent or more) be devoted directly to the active conduct of the charitable activities of the POF. Charitable use assets include the art, assuming it is on display or loan (and not just held for investment), and any museum exhibition building, so this test should not be difficult to meet in most cases. Where problems may arise is when art owned by the POF is either directly or indirectly used by the collector for personal benefit. If the art is not housed in a separate location but is loaned out to other charitable organizations, it is essential that the art not be used or displayed by the collector in his or her own home when not otherwise exhibited.

The endowment test requires a direct distribution of two-thirds of the POF's minimum investment return (defined as 5 percent of its investment assets)—that is, 3.33 percent of the POF's investment assets—for its charitable purposes. For all practical purposes, a POF that satisfies the income test will meet the endowment test.

The support test is dependent on fund-raising and, therefore, would rarely be used by a POF established by a collector (or by an artist-funded foundation, as discussed below).

Although somewhat technical, these tests are not difficult to meet for a collector who wishes to establish his or her own museum. However, the nontax aspects of establishing and operating one's own museum may outweigh the tax benefits and the control retained over the collection that are available by using a POF. In addition to the value of the collection, which should be considerable for someone to consider establishing a museum, the costs to build and operate an appropriate facility to house valuable art are significant. The collector should be fully informed as to the costs to build, maintain, and operate the museum, including the cost of curation and security. In other words, they need a well-thought-out business plan before embarking on this course.

need business plan

Collectors who are considering establishing a POF should also be aware that private museums have come under increased scrutiny in recent years. In particular, the first draft of the legislation that eventually became the 2017 Tax Act included a provision requiring private art museums to be open to the public for at least 1,000 hours each year. This provision does

only "new" ? end up in prior Law.

→ POF museums must be open to public at least 1000 hours/year

not appear in the final legislation, but its inclusion in the early draft indicates that a concern exists among some legislators and regulators that this is an area of potential abuse, which may result in future attempts to further regulate the formation and operation of private museums.

Collectors who are considering a private museum should be aware that there are several recent articles on the topic.[10]

POFs are increasingly being used by artists to preserve their legacy and to manage inventory that may be on hand at their death. This topic is discussed further in part 5.

It is also possible to create and use a private nonoperating foundation as part of an overall planning structure. The federal income tax charitable deduction for donations of art during life will be limited to cost basis as opposed to fair market value. Furthermore, the collector who creates a private nonoperating foundation will be severely limited in their activities with respect to art contributed to the foundation because of private foundation excise taxes enacted to deter errant behavior, including self-dealing. As a result, it is more likely that a private nonoperating foundation would be formed at death—or at least receive art contributions at death.

International Charitable Giving

Increasingly, donors are interested in contributing financial assets or art to foreign museums. This has been particularly true in recent years as Asian museums have grown in size and number and have focused on bringing Asian art back from the Western world. A full discussion of international charitable giving is beyond the scope of this book, but donors interested in giving to a foreign museum should be aware that they must comply with any rules and regulations pertaining to the international nature of the transaction, such as tariffs and duties. They also must keep in mind the following tax considerations.

Charitable gifts of any type to foreign charities are generally not deductible for U.S. federal income tax purposes. This is true whether the donation is made in financial assets or with art. However, other planning options exist that may enable the donor to accomplish their goal of transferring artwork to a foreign museum in a tax-efficient manner.

The first step is to determine if there is a tax treaty between the United States and the foreign country that may specifically address the federal income tax treatment of contributions by U.S. citizens to charities located in that particular foreign country. It is unlikely that a treaty exists; however, that should always be the starting point in any foreign transaction.

One option is to donate the art outright to the foreign museum, forgoing any federal income tax charitable deduction.

A second option is to enter into a bargain sale, selling the art to the museum for a price equal to the donor's cost basis in the art. This would result in no income to the donor, no economic loss to the donor, and no federal income tax charitable deduction to the donor. This would require the foreign museum to be willing and able to pay the bargain price for the art.

A third option is to donate the art to a "friends of" organization that is a U.S.-based charitable organization and that would in turn transfer the art to the foreign museum. Since this type of donation would likely fail the related-use test, the donor would be limited to a cost-basis deduction for federal income tax purposes. Donors should be aware that if the "friends of" organization is deemed to be a "mere conduit," then no charitable deduction will be allowed. This is a highly technical issue that counsel should explore with the "friends of" organization prior to any donation being made.

A fourth option exists if the donor has a private foundation. In that case, the donor can contribute the art to their private foundation and receive a cost-basis deduction for federal income tax purposes (because the donated asset is not publicly traded stock, as discussed above). The private foundation can subsequently distribute the artwork to the foreign museum, after conducting what is known as expenditure responsibility. Assuming this is conducted appropriately, the distribution by the private foundation to the foreign charity will count toward the private foundation's distribution requirement.

A fifth option may exist as well, and that is to contribute the art to a "friends of" organization specifically aligned with a foreign museum that is not deemed to be a "mere conduit" under the rules mentioned above. That would entitle the donor to a full fair market value charitable deduction for federal income tax purposes, subject to the other rules discussed above.

Finally, it may be possible to contribute the artwork to a U.S.-based museum that has a lending relationship with a foreign museum. In that case, the donor would contribute the artwork to the U.S. museum and receive a full fair market value deduction for federal income tax purposes. The U.S. museum could then lend the artwork to the foreign museum.

The above is a general discussion of options to consider when transferring artwork to a foreign museum. Many technical rules exist, and it is incumbent upon the donor and the donor's advisory team to closely examine those rules vis-à-vis their particular fact situation to ensure compliance with all applicable rules.

Summary

A sale of art during life is probably the most expensive sale that the collector will ever make, and a gift of art to family (or other noncharitable beneficiary) during life is likely the least efficient form of wealth transfer, leaving a donation of art to charity as the most tax-efficient way to preserve a collection. This is, of course, subject to the collector's desires, including the desires of the family or other intended beneficiaries.

Notes

1. Treas. Reg. § 1.170A-4(b)(3)(i).
2. There are few litigated cases on what constitutes a "related use." However, there are a number of private letter rulings on the topic. *See, e.g.*, I.R.S. Priv. Ltr. Ruls. 77-51-044, 79-11-109, and 79-34-082, finding that the display of lithographs in a camp and center devoted to children with disabilities satisfied the related-use requirement as it advanced the purpose of an art appreciation program; I.R.S. Priv. Ltr. Rul. 81-43-029, finding that the donation of a collection of porcelain art furthered the mission of a suitable living environment in a retirement center; and I.R.S. Priv. Ltr. Rul. 98-33-011, finding that paintings contributed to a Jewish community center met the related-use requirement where the center had an arts wing and library. Chapter 15 of Ralph E. Lerner & Judith Bresler, Art Law (Practising Law Inst., 4th ed. 2012) includes other examples.
3. IRC § 170(f)(3)(A).

4. Richard M. Horwood, *Key Issues for Collectors: Working with Museums,* 13 Fam. Found. Advisor, no. 3, Mar./Apr. 2014.

5. Treas. Reg. § 1.170A-7(b)(1)(i).

6. IRC § 170(a)(3).

7. IRC § 170(e)(1)(B).

8. Rather than cite each particular code section or regulation section, I refer you to Jerry J. McCoy & Kathryn W. Miree, Family Foundation Handbook § 2.06[A] (CCH 2013), and Lerner & Bresler, Art Law, *supra* note 2, at 1297–1300. These in turn will refer you to IRC § 4942 and the regulations thereunder that govern the formation of private operating foundations. *See also* Richard M. Horwood, Kenneth A. Goldstein & Chelsey E. Ziegler, *Private Operating Foundations: The Hands-on Approach to a Charitable Legacy,* 13 Fam. Found. Advisor, no. 5, July/Aug. 2014.

9. Katherine E. David, *The Ins and Outs of Private Operating Foundations,* 17 Fam. Found. Advisor, no. 2, Jan./Feb. 2018, provides a history of the provisions related to POFs and provides a number of calculation examples.

10. Horwood, Goldstein & Ziegler, *supra* note 8; Michael Shnayerson, *Inside the Private Museums of Billionaire Art Collectors,* Town & Country, Jan. 16, 2017.

12

Selling—At Death

The remaining options that should be explored are those that take effect upon the death of the collector (or perhaps at the death of the surviving spouse in the case of a collector couple).

Selling art at the death of the collector is likely the most common scenario. This may be by design or simply because the collector could not or would not part with the art while alive—or even engage in the planning process while alive.

From a purely tax planning point of view, the biggest advantage to selling art at the collector's death is that the cost basis in the art will be stepped up to its fair market value.[1] As a result, the 28 percent long-term capital gains rate for collectibles and the 3.8 percent health-care surtax are not relevant except for post-death, presale appreciation. In fact, with the now larger AEA, for most people a sale at death, rather than a sale during life, will provide the best overall tax outcome. No capital gains tax, health-care surtax, or transfer tax will be due. This will also mean that the collector is able to retain, and enjoy, the collection throughout their life.

The biggest drawback to selling at death is not tax related; rather, it is the fact that the person who knew the most about the collection is no longer around. This can lead to major issues—inventory of items, provenance, network of dealers and galleries familiar with the collection—if meticulous records have not been maintained. Furthermore, the personal representative of the estate will need to be knowledgeable about the art or able to retain someone who is. Otherwise, the art may be sold for much less than its actual worth. In fact, if the decision is made during life that a sale will be made at death, it is a best practice to make arrangements with the appropriate parties—auction houses or galleries—while the collector is alive. Given the substantial transaction costs that may be incurred, the collector (or collector's advisors) will be in the best position to negotiate reduced sellers' premiums.

The author is aware of an estate where the collector not only maintained meticulous records but also had encrypted those records! No one who worked on the matter could figure out the code; in fact, the only person alive who knew the code was a former, somewhat disgruntled employee, now perhaps in a position to take advantage of her special knowledge. So while detailed records are always helpful, make sure someone knows where they are and can actually understand them.

If a recent appraisal is not available, it will be necessary for the collection to be appraised if the estate is above the AEA because an appraisal will have to be filed with Form 706, Federal Estate Tax Return.[2] Even if an appraisal is not required, it is still good practice to have an appraisal prepared to give the personal representative an idea of what the pieces should be sold for. With or without an appraisal, Revenue Procedure 65-19 provides that a public sale of art or collectibles within a reasonable period of time after the collector's death sets the fair market value for purposes of estate taxes. Interestingly, the revenue procedure also requires that any buyer's premium paid at a public auction be considered as part of the value of the art even though the buyer's premium is paid to the auction house, not the estate.[3] The premium can then be deducted under section 2053 if the sale is deemed necessary for the payment of estate expenses. See the discussion below regarding how to ensure that this deduction is available.

If the art is being sold at death, it is included in the estate and subjected to the federal estate tax system and a 40 percent federal estate tax rate (plus any applicable state estate taxes) above the AEA. This can give rise to liquidity issues, depending on the makeup of the whole estate, as some or all of the art may need to be sold to provide liquidity to pay estate taxes and other costs of maintaining the collection during estate administration or to make cash bequests or other distributions.

Case Study

A collector, widowed with two adult daughters, owned a painting worth $12 million and had approximately $6 million in liquid assets. Under today's federal estate tax system, her estate would owe approximately $2 million in federal estate taxes (plus any state estate taxes and other costs of estate administration). This would leave the estate with a $12 million painting and $4 million in liquidity. The latter would be easy to divide, but the former could become a nightmare.

It is important that the collector's estate documents (will or revocable trust) have appropriate language to support a deduction for any expenses incurred to sell the collection, in whole or in part. Expenses incurred by the estate to sell art are deductible if the sale is necessary to pay debts, expenses, or taxes; to preserve the estate; or to effect distribution.[4] A provision should be included in the estate planning documents that directs that any art not bequeathed or selected by beneficiaries be sold and proceeds distributed. This should be sufficient to establish that the sale was necessary to effect a distribution of estate assets, thereby ensuring the availability of the deduction under section 2053.

In any case, the executor will need to elect whether to deduct these expenses on the federal estate tax return or the estate's fiduciary income tax return.

Estate Administration

Although storing and insuring the art is important at all stages of the collection, it becomes critically important during estate administration. This is true whether the art is sold, gifted to family members or others, or donated to charity. There will be a period of time between the death of the collector and the ultimate disposition of the collection when the estate representative will be held to the highest standard of conduct to ensure that the value of the collection is preserved for the benefit of the estate and its beneficiaries. The personal representative must be especially on guard against the disappearance of small but valuable items. The best means to prevent this outright theft by those who have access to the collection—well intentioned or not—is for the collector to make sure the inventory is up-to-date, reflecting all sales and purchases on an ongoing basis.

The degree of care will, of course, be dependent on the collection. In some cases, it may be appropriate for the collection to stay where it is—for example, where the surviving spouse is the estate representative and the sole heir to the collection. In other cases, it may be prudent for the estate representative to have the collection packed and shipped to an appropriate storage facility pending the outcome of estate proceedings and final distribution of the pieces, regardless of whether they are being sold, gifted, or donated.

Specialists exist for each step of the process, from packing, to transporting, to storing in climate-controlled and secure facilities, to completing restoration work prior to sale or donation. Local museums are a great source of information to help the estate representative determine appropriate professionals for each of these services.

In addition to the physical handling of the collection, it will be necessary to obtain appropriate appraisals, as discussed in chapter 4.

The actual sales process was described in chapter 9.

Summary

Although a sale at death is perhaps the most common outcome, and perhaps the best outcome from a combined federal tax point of view, it is potentially the most difficult option if the collector has not planned for this outcome. It is important that a qualified personal representative be used, one who is knowledgeable about art, and that appropriate documentation about the collection be prepared for use by the personal representative.

Notes

1. IRC § 1014.
2. *See* chapter 4 regarding appraisal requirements.
3. Rev. Proc. 65-19, 1965-2 C.B. 1002.
4. Treas. Reg. § 20.2053-3(d)(2).

13

Gifting (Bequeathing)— At Death

Is it the art or is it the money?

Again, we need to start with the question of whether the family wants to maintain the art. If so, then certain planning approaches are preferable to those used when the family does not share the collector's passion for the art and is interested only in the wealth represented by the art.

Case Study

A collector had built a collection of contemporary art, including several significant works. The collector was operating under the assumption that upon his death the collection would simply be divided among his three children as they agreed among themselves. However, one child was an avid collector himself and had particular interest in several of his father's pieces. The other children did not especially care for the art (beyond its value). Conflict in the making!

The starting point for the solution was a current appraisal, which arrived at a value of the total collection (62 pieces) of $28 million, with most of that value represented by four pieces. It was going to be difficult to equitably divide the collection and the value of the collection. Among the various solutions presented, the father chose a relatively simple solution: at death, the collection (and individual pieces) would be appraised

---

(which would be required for purposes of filing a Form 706, Federal Estate Tax Return), the collector child would have the right to choose whatever pieces he wanted, and equalizing distributions would be made to the other children from other assets.

This case study demonstrates several issues. First, this estate would have enough "other assets" for equalizing distributions. That is not always the situation. Second, issues arise where one child has superior knowledge as to the value of pieces. Here, that was solved with an appraisal and a mandated distribution priority. Finally, nothing beats preplanning! Other planning options may have made this process even easier on everyone involved.

From a federal estate tax point of view, the art is included in the estate at its then fair market value, and its cost basis is stepped up to that fair market value. If the art is to be sold, then consideration should be given to the topics discussed in the previous chapter.

Estate administration, of course, is important, and the considerations discussed in chapter 12 should be taken into account. In addition, the following should be considered.

There are two basic ways to complete an estate plan: using a will with dispositive provisions and using a pour-over will and revocable trust with dispositive provisions in the revocable trust. In either case, the general pattern of estate disposition is "A-B funding," with the "A" share representing the amount of the marital share (assuming there is a surviving spouse) and the "B" share representing the unused AEA. As with other planning techniques, there are many variations on this theme, and this has perhaps only become more complicated with the addition of portability of the AEA to the transfer tax system and the significant increase to the AEA. Portability is not particularly germane to our discussion, so I will not discuss it further.

Nor will I discuss all of the variations on a theme of A-B planning because most often art and other tangible personal property are disposed of not via the A-B funding but rather through an outright disposition. I will discuss some trust options below that apply, regardless of whether or not the art is disposed of as part of A-B funding.

Back to the basic structure of the estate plan. For collectors, it is often advisable to use the revocable trust structure and actually transfer their art, or interests in an LLC owning art, to the revocable trust. Note that this is not the same as establishing a gift trust, as discussed in chapter 10, which is fairly cumbersome. While probate is not a particularly cumbersome process in the author's home state, it is an expensive process in many states, and using a funded revocable trust will minimize the impact of probate. Furthermore, to the extent that a collector wishes to maintain privacy regarding the collection, particularly the value of the collection, then using a funded revocable trust will help greatly in this regard. During life, the collector maintains complete control of and flexibility concerning the art and can provide for successor management should the collector become incapacitated. The revocable trust will also allow the successor trustee to make decisions with respect to management of the art without probate court involvement.

The revocable trust becomes irrevocable at the death of the collector and can control the disposition of the collector's art. To the extent that disposition is directed over certain pieces, these directions can be changed much more easily during the collector's life by amending a revocable trust than by amending a will (by codicil or a new will).

The revocable trust will not accomplish any tax planning in and of itself. Rather, estate tax minimization techniques that can be incorporated into a will can simply be incorporated into the revocable trust structure.

Whether in a will or revocable trust, a bequest of art should be clear and unambiguous to avoid conflicts among beneficiaries, as would likely have happened in the case study above. A bequest of art "in equal shares" will more often than not lead to disputes among beneficiaries. Likewise, leaving the decision to the personal representative as to how to divvy up the art will probably lead to disputes.

Perhaps a better solution is to leave specific items to specific beneficiaries or to provide that beneficiaries will have the right to select items of art as they wish, with the balance to be sold. There may even be a process to determine an order of selection—say, oldest child gets first choice, then second oldest, and so on—with equalizing distributions made from other assets. Think of this as a private auction, although no money actually changes hands. This is the author's preferred method, though other methods may be employed as well.

Some question exists as to the proper federal estate tax treatment when a surviving spouse is included in this process. Normally, if something is left to a surviving spouse, the estate is entitled to a marital deduction for the value of whatever passes to the surviving spouse outright or in certain qualifying trusts. However, whatever passes to the surviving spouse cannot be a "terminable interest" except where it is to a "qualified terminable interest property trust," commonly known as a QTIP trust.[1]

If the surviving spouse is given, in effect, a first right of refusal to select among the artwork, there is some question as to whether that is a terminable interest. If so, then the marital deduction would not be available, even for art that the surviving spouse actually selected, which could be an unpleasant surprise at best—and an estate tax tsunami at worst.

To avoid this issue, it is best to make a specific bequest of the items to go to the surviving spouse. If, however, the collector gives the surviving spouse a right of first refusal, this should be limited to the time period permitted for a qualified disclaimer (another topic that will not be addressed herein—but generally nine months after the date of death); then the marital deduction will still be available for items passing to the surviving spouse. The author is not aware of any cases where a surviving spouse was given the option to choose items for a period of time longer than the disclaimer period. Hence, the drafter of the estate documents should consider limiting any such time period to make a choice to the same time period allowed for a qualified disclaimer.

Perhaps a better option is—subject to other planning that may be in place, such as an LLC that owns the art—to make a bequest of all of the art to the surviving spouse and enable the surviving spouse to make a qualified disclaimer under IRC § 2518 of any pieces that he or she does not want. The greatest challenges with this option, just as with any disclaimer planning, are to ensure, first, that the surviving spouse does not take any action within the disclaimer period that would disqualify the disclaimer and, second, that any required action is taken within the disclaimer time period. Since we are dealing with tangible personal property, likely located in the home, this is much more difficult than would be the case with intangible assets, such as stocks and bonds. So is it possible to do this planning? Yes, but the author thinks it is somewhat risky—not technically but from a practical point of view.

[handwritten note: have it all been re-titled?]

Trust Structures

The above assumes an outright distribution of the art to the beneficiaries. However, depending on the overall makeup of the collector's estate and the extent of lifetime planning, it may be that a disposition at death will include transfers to trusts established during life or to new trusts created within the will or revocable trust structure. In such case, several important decisions need to be made.

If the makeup of the collector's estate is such that it will be necessary or desirable to include the art in the A-B funding, then it will almost always make sense to use the art to fund the "B" trust, as art tends to be the type of asset—appreciating but with no steady income—that is better for funding the "B" share rather than the "A" share.

If a trust will continue to own art, then all of the considerations discussed in chapter 10 in the section "Trust Structures" should be considered. If a trust is used, it is imperative to "retitle" the art to the trust, and the change in ownership should be reflected on insurance policies and inventories. Physical possession of the art must be considered. If beneficiaries are allowed to possess and display the art, then the trustee must confirm that appropriate insurance coverage is in place, that the beneficiaries' residence or other place of display is appropriately secure, and that other risk-management practices are being followed. And, of course, sufficient liquid assets need to be funded to the trust as well to ensure the trustee's ability to continue to pay expenses associated with the art.

Several commentators have suggested the use of a purpose trust to hold tangible personal property. A purpose trust exists to carry out a specific purpose, not to benefit the trust beneficiaries. The author has not worked with a purpose trust established to own art but suggests that advisors wishing more information may wish to consult articles available on this topic.[2]

[handwritten note: look into a purpose trust.]

Summary

Once again, it is best to plan. A general disposition to spouse and other heirs, as they decide, may be an easy out for the collector, but it is sure to cause delays and ill will among family members for years to come. It will also add unnecessary expense. In short, avoid this at all costs!

Have a plan. And name a personal representative with enough famil-iarity with your art so that the plan can be carried out in a cost-effective and time-efficient manner. And leave information about the art—more precisely, an up-to-date inventory—so that the personal representative knows what they are dealing with.

Notes

1. IRC § 2056 outlines the requirements for the federal estate tax marital deduction.

2. Wendy S. Goffe, *Estate Planning for Liquid Assets of the Vintage Varietal*, STEVE LEIMBERG'S EST. PLAN. NEWSL., no. 2173, Dec. 8, 2013, discusses planning for wine collections. The article mentions purpose trusts and further refers the reader to Alexander A. Bove, Jr., *The Purpose of Purpose Trusts*, PROB. & PROP., May/June 2004, at 34. *See also* Alexander A. Bove, Jr., & Ruth Mattson, *The Pur-pose Trust: Drafting Becomes a Work of Art*, 43 EST. PLAN. J., no. 10, Oct. 2016.

14

Donating—At Death

Donating art to charity at death is a much simpler process, at least from a federal tax point of view, than donating during life. All of the special federal income tax charitable deduction rules discussed in chapter 11 do not apply to testamentary donations. Individual pieces or the entire collection—whatever the collector decides and has stated in the will or other estate planning documents—is delivered to the institution, and the collector's estate receives a federal estate tax deduction equal to the then value of the artwork. The amount of the deduction will, of course, require an ascertainable value and must be supported by an appropriate appraisal, as discussed in chapter 4.

Just as with sales and bequests to family at death, the advantage of waiting until death to transfer the artwork to charity is that the collector gets to continue to possess and enjoy the artwork during life.

From a federal tax planning point of view, the biggest drawback of waiting until death to give art to charity is that the collector forfeits the federal income tax charitable deduction that would have been available if the art had been donated during life. For a married couple, one way around this is for the first spouse to leave the collection to the surviving spouse and then have the surviving spouse donate the collection. The transfer to the surviving spouse will be free of federal estate tax because of the unlimited marital deduction, and the surviving spouse will be entitled to a federal income tax charitable deduction, subject to the limitations discussed in chapter 11.

Just as with lifetime donations, it is important that the collector specify any special conditions either in the will or other estate planning documents or, better yet, in an agreement reached with the institution during life. Will the art become part of the museum's general collection, or will it maintain a separate identity? Can the art be sold? Will it be on permanent display? Is the museum permitted to lend the art to other institutions? Will additional funds be required to maintain the collection? These conditions can, and should, be negotiated up front while the collector is alive even if the art will not actually be delivered until after the collector's death. Care must be taken that the conditions are acceptable to both the collector and the institution and are not so restrictive as to jeopardize the federal estate tax charitable deduction. Absent such an agreement, it is possible that the charity named in the will or other estate planning documents might reject the donation.

The simplest way to donate art to charity at death is a direct donation. However, certain of the other techniques discussed in chapter 11, regarding donations during life, are also available for donations of art at death. These would include bargain sales (enhanced because of the basis step-up at death) and even loans if the estate documents empower the personal representative to enter into, or continue, loans of the art. Also, certain charitable planning techniques that do not work particularly well during life—because of the federal income tax charitable deduction rules or because of simple economics—may work well for donations taking effect at death.

Charitable remainder trusts (CRTs), discussed in chapter 11, are problematic if created at death, just as if created during life, but for slightly different reasons. Testamentary CRTs do not face the problems of the related-use rule (causing a cost-basis limit on the federal income tax charitable deduction) or the delayed (until sale) federal income tax charitable deduction encountered with lifetime (inter vivos) CRTs. But the problem still remains that the CRT trustee must be able to invest in income-producing assets. Therefore, testamentary CRTs make sense only when a sale of a portion or all of the collection is contemplated.

Charitable lead trusts (CLTs), briefly mentioned in chapter 11, are perhaps more useful if established at death than during life when funded with art. A CLT pays an income stream (either annuity or unitrust) to charity for a set term. That term may be a term of years or for the life or lives of named individuals. At the end of the income term, any assets remaining in the CLT pass to one or more noncharitable beneficiaries, usually family members.

A CLT can be useful as a testamentary planning tool. The CLT can be structured to provide the collector's estate with an immediate estate tax charitable deduction for the full value of the art placed in the CLT. Assuming that the trustee of the CLT sells the art shortly after funding, reinvests the proceeds, and earns an investment return in excess of the section 7520 rate in effect at the time of funding, any such excess earnings will pass transfer tax free to the collector's named CLT beneficiaries.

It should be noted that using either CRTs or CLTs in this context contemplates a sale of the art rather than a donation of the art to charity. As such, these are more tax-savings techniques rather than pure art planning.

Private operating foundations, discussed in chapter 11, can also be established at death, though it is preferable to establish the POF during life even if most of the funding occurs at death. A lifetime transfer allows the collector to receive a federal income tax charitable deduction and, perhaps more importantly, to be alive to see their dream come true! The use of a POF by an artist is discussed in chapter 19.

If a collection is to be donated to a private nonoperating foundation, it is preferable to do so at death. A federal income tax charitable deduction for a donation during life will be limited to cost basis; this will not matter if the donation is made at death. Furthermore, it may be easier to avoid the imposition of the various excise taxes applicable to private foundations after the donor's death. Finally, the lending of art by the foundation to museums and other public charities will be considered to be part of the 5 percent minimum required payout of the foundation, and the value of the artwork itself will not be considered in the calculation of how much must be distributed by the foundation each year.

Finally, the discussion on estate administration in chapter 12 again pertains to donations of art at death. It is likely that some period of time will pass between the collector's death and the disposition of the art, be it by sale or by transfer to family or to charity. The personal representative of the collector's estate must be mindful of their duties to protect and preserve the art during the time it is under their care.

Summary

A charitable donation at death allows the collector to continue to enjoy the art for the rest of their life. However, this comes at the cost of losing any federal income tax charitable deduction.

For both lifetime and testamentary donations, just as important as the tax benefits to be achieved is the absolute need to agree with the recipient organization on the intended use and display parameters of the art to be donated.

PART 4

Putting It All Together

Now that we know our options, let's look at several fact patterns and suggested solutions. Remember that it is important to consider every possible solution each time. It is also important to remember that the options, although exhaustive, are not mutually exclusive and that collectors will almost always use multiple options.

15

Additional Planning Examples

Working with collectors and their advisors exposes a planner to a broad array of fact patterns, some good and some not so good. Many case studies are included in the preceding chapters. I share the following to illustrate the breadth of issues that one encounters when advising art collectors. Some of these case studies have rather obvious fact patterns and solutions; others present issues that one might not consider but that are very real—especially if they happen to you!

I invite you to share your client experiences with me for inclusion in any subsequent editions of this book.

Case Studies—Risk Management

A collector displayed his collection of Master oils on the first floor of his residence, which had been designed around the display of the collection. This, by the way, is common practice, and many collector clients design and build their homes primarily to display their collection.

This home and the collection were well known in the town in which they were situated—so much so that when the local fire department was dispatched in response to a fire alarm, great care was taken by fire department personnel to remove the paintings from the downstairs while other firefighters were extinguishing the fire upstairs. The entire collection was saved and removed to the front yard while the fire was extinguished.

The paintings, of course, had soot and ash deposited on them. Professional art restorers are usually chemists by training and/or practice and are experienced in how to remove soot and ash and minimize damage. The collector, however, was not trained in this specialized area. Seeing his collection exposed like that, he frantically started to wipe the soot and ash off of the paintings with a wet towel. The problem? The water actually acted as a catalyst to the chemicals in the soot and ash, thereby causing further damage that could have mostly been avoided by a professional.

Lesson: Don't try art restoration at home!

* * *

A collector was rearranging the display of his collection in his primary residence. While moving paintings around, many were set on the floor, leaning against the walls, until rehung. This exposed the valuable oil paintings to energetic grandchildren, with feet and elbows, and even more so to happy dogs wagging their tails against the paintings!

Case Studies—Art Lending

A collector borrowed $32 million, secured by his art collection, to purchase an interest in a professional sports team. The collector otherwise had access to financing but felt this was the best source of financing given his options and his overall financial situation.

* * *

A collector with an extensive modern art collection obtained a $12.5 million line of credit, secured by his art collection, to (1) provide additional working capital for his business and (2) have immediate liquidity to purchase additional art.

* * *

A collector purchased a new estate property that required extensive renovation before it could become her personal residence. Rather than borrow against her investment portfolio, the collector chose to borrow against her collection of early American paintings to complete the renovation, where most of the collection is now placed.

* * *

A collector whose wealth was concentrated in real estate and fine art desired to diversify his investments. The collection was appraised at $80 million, which allowed the collector to borrow $40 million to diversify investments and to add several significant pieces to his collection.

* * *

A collector borrowed against his collection and used the funds to purchase life insurance to provide liquidity to his estate. The inherent arbitrage made possible by the use of life insurance in this situation effectively reduced the collector's estate tax rate by half.

These examples show the various uses of art loans beyond the acquisition of more art. In fact, the majority of art loans are used for purposes other than art acquisition.

Case Studies—Planning

A collector of contemporary art had a general bequest in her will leaving her tangible personal property equally to her three children. One child was a collector herself and was interested in specific pieces in her mother's collection, while the others were not. This would invariably lead to conflict among the children, especially given the significant value of the collection. It was likely that one child would want to retain as much of the collection as possible, while the others would likely be inclined to sell the collection or receive other assets in lieu of the art.

The collector revised her will to leave specific pieces to the child who expressed an interest in those specific pieces, while the other children would receive additional financial assets to equalize the value that each child received.

* * *

A collector moved his collection from his primary residence to the family's vacation home so that the entire family could enjoy the collection. The collector desired that the family maintain the collection after he passed away, as a family legacy. Rather than giving individual pieces to family members, the entire collection was transferred to an LLC. In this way, transferring the collection was simplified by transferring LLC interests to family members during life and at the collector's death rather than by either fractionalizing individual pieces or giving individual pieces to various family members. Future decisions regarding the collection will be made at the LLC level, including whether to buy or sell art.

This is not a "perfect" solution, as decisions will still require at least a majority vote; however, the collector felt this was the best alternative for maintaining the collection.

put the art into an LLC

* * *

A collector accumulated a significant sculpture collection valued at $100 million. Confident that her family would otherwise be financially secure, she had initially decided to build a museum to house her collection. However, after discussing the costs to build and maintain a museum, the collector determined that a better, more efficient course of action would be to donate the collection to an existing museum with similar art. The collector, with her advisors, located such a museum and crafted a donation agreement specifying the terms and conditions of the donation and the parameters for the display and maintenance of the collection. The donation was structured to occur during her life and, over time, to maximize the federal income tax benefits to her. The collector has in addition made a significant cash gift to help endow additional costs of maintaining her collection.

* * *

A supporter of museum-based art education programs, as well as several nonprofit educational institutions, owns an extensive range of fine art. His plan was to divide the collection, at death, among the nonprofit institutions and museums that he worked with during life.

Reviewing his entire financial situation, it was determined that a better course of action was to make a lifetime financial gift to one of the nonprofits and donate a portion of the collection to one of the museums, with a resulting income tax deduction and reduced estate tax liability exposure. In addition to the tax efficiency of this plan, the collector was able to share a portion of his collection with a larger audience during his life.

* * *

A collector owned a substantial collection, worth in excess of $125 million, of impressionist art. She had no children, and her more distant heirs were not interested in art. There were no museums in her locality that were willing to accept a donation of the art with her stipulation that it be on view in perpetuity. The collector determined that accomplishing that goal would require either seeking out other museums outside of her geographic locale, which she did not want to do, or establishing her own museum.

* * *

A collector converted an existing structure to house her museum and has made other resources available to endow its continued operation. The museum is now open to the public, and given the quality of both the collection and the facility, several other collectors are considering making donations of their complementary collections to the museum.

* * *

At the end of 2012, there was a mad rush to use the $5 million AEA before its expiration on December 31 of that year. As it turns out, the mad rush was not necessary, as the exemption amount was made permanent and indexed for inflation (at least until the next round of changes!).

During the latter half of 2012, a number of collectors sought to use the exemption but not use liquid assets to fund the gift, whether it was outright or in trust. Many collectors decided that art would be a good asset to give, as it would not affect their liquidity. Remember that the first question is always, Does the family share your interest in the art? For this group of people, the answer was usually "I have no idea."

For better (or worse), the next part of their plan usually involved keeping the art at their residence by renting it back from the family (or entity set up to hold the art) on the theory that the art was best protected by remaining where it was.

This planning scenario, as discussed in chapter 10, is fraught with tax and other issues. It also points out the difference between wealth-transfer planning with art and planning with art. The former focuses on the value of the art; the latter focuses on the art itself.

Disclaimer

The case studies are presented for illustration and do not necessarily reflect specific strategies that may have been developed for these collectors. They are for illustrative purposes only. They are certainly not intended to serve as specific tax advice, since the availability and effectiveness of any strategy are dependent on your individual facts and circumstances. Results will vary, and no suggestion is made about how any specific solution or strategy performed in reality.

16

Summary: Collectors

Hopefully, you have found portions or all of the preceding chapters helpful to you as a collector or as someone who advises collectors. And hopefully you have found the case studies to be helpful—or at least enjoyable.

I often speak and write on this topic and have been asked to list the three most important points about planning with art. Rather than responding with three, I thought that since we live in an age of "Top Ten" lists, I would compile one of my own. So before we get to the topic of planning specific to artists, here's my "Top Ten" list for collectors:

1. *Plan.* Do not leave the disposition of your collection to chance.
2. *Use competent and experienced advisors.* Use a complete and competent advisory team. Professionals always say that but often do not follow their own advice. The team should include art experts, such as dealers, gallery owners, curators, and restoration experts; risk-management professionals; qualified appraisers; private bankers; and attorneys and accountants—all with experience in planning with art. Not only do they need to be on your advisory team, but also they need to communicate with one another.
3. *Do appropriate risk management.* Engage an insurance expert who is specifically experienced with art. You may or may not purchase insurance, but do consider the security of your collection from theft, fire, water, storm, or other casualties.

4. *Prepare and maintain an inventory.* This is true for all assets, but it is particularly true with respect to art and other collectibles. The particulars of an inventory are discussed in chapter 3. This inventory is critical to every stage of the planning process and should be kept as current as possible.

5. *Know the value of your collection.* Insurance providers and lenders, if any, will require appraisals and periodic updates. Appraisals will be required for implementing most of the planning ideas herein. Even if not required, you should have your collection periodically valued, perhaps every three to five years, depending on how actively you are collecting and on what you are collecting.

6. *Maintain records.* As part of your inventory, maintain records of ownership and, as the value and significance of the collection grow, further evidence of provenance. This includes all contracts to purchase or sell, actual bills of sale, loan agreements with museums, and so on. Consider title insurance if you have doubts about the provenance of any piece you are considering for purchase.

7. *Ask the Big Question.* Involve your family. Do they share your passion for your art? If so, planning should focus on how to transition the art to them, whether that is now or later. If not, and there are other financial assets or you feel they are otherwise provided for, then explore your charitable options.

8. *Consider charity.* Given the expense of selling and the opportunity cost of wealth transfer, the "charitable solution" is often the most tax-efficient way to keep your collection intact. And if the "charitable solution" is right for you, consider donations during life, as this will entitle you to a federal income tax charitable deduction in addition to estate tax savings. Most important, do not surprise museums (or other charities) if you are leaving art to them. Not all museums will want your art. It may not fit their collections or their storage vaults. Talk to them now about your wishes even if they are not carried out until later.

9. *No surprises.* Give your family and your personal representative clear direction on what your estate will include and clear direction on what you want to happen. And while you are going through the

planning process, make sure your advisors know the extent and value of your collection.

10. *Enjoy!* Difficult as it may seem, try to enjoy the process of planning for the disposition of your collection. It is certainly not as much fun as building the collection, but it is ultimately just as important.

PART 5

Planning for Artists

An increasing number of artists have achieved commercial success since the latter part of the 20th century. Prior to that time, tax and financial planning was not particularly important to them; now, tax and financial planning may be as important to the commercially successful artist as preserving their artist legacy.

This part of the book, focusing on the commercially successful artist, will follow the same format as the rest of the book; that is, it will focus on planning during life (chapter 17) and planning at death (chapter 18), and it will examine the options of selling, gifting to family (or other noncharitable beneficiary), and donating to charity. Most of the same considerations will apply, so reference is made back to the earlier parts of the book. Chapter 19 will examine the use of artist-funded foundations, which have grown in popularity as an increasing number of artists have achieved commercial success.

The focus in this part will be on the artist's self-created work, not on collections of other artists' works that they may have acquired themselves. To the extent that an artist has built a collection of other artists' works, then all of the considerations discussed in parts 1–4 of this book apply to their collection.

17

Planning During Life

Planning for artists involves two special considerations, their artistic legacy and, from a legal, tax, and financial planning point of view, the fact that their self-created work is ordinary income property, or inventory—not a capital asset, as it is for collectors and investors.

An artist's legacy is paramount to them. Their work, regardless of medium, reflects their worldview. It may be influenced in varying degrees by their view of nature, humankind, politics, religion, and other social interactions. It is both very personal to them and very important to them. Planners need to remember this whenever discussing any tax and financial plan, as the artist's legacy will be paramount in any solutions acceptable to them.

Although the art or other collectible may have the same physical characteristics in the artist's hands as in the collector's hands, it is a different asset for legal and tax purposes. For collectors (and investors), art is a capital asset; for artists, self-created works are ordinary income property, also known as inventory, which leads to different tax outcomes. The three chapters devoted to artists will focus on this important distinction.

Selling During Life

For artists, selling during life is fairly straightforward. Self-created work is inventory. As such, proceeds from the sale of their art are ordinary income. The actual costs of materials, studio rental, and any other ordinary, necessary, and reasonable expenses are deductible from income as paid (assuming they are cash-basis taxpayers).

Several other considerations must be taken into account, a full discussion of which is beyond the scope of this book:

- Collection and remittance of sales or use tax to state and local taxing authorities.
- Selection of business entity, which may be a sole proprietorship, a partnership if working with one or more other artists, a limited liability company, or a regular ("C") or pass-through ("S") corporation. Although not discussed further here, this is an important decision for the commercially successful artist to make, especially since the passage of the 2017 Tax Act, as the difference in applicable federal and state income tax rates can be significant. Furthermore, the use of an appropriate business entity may assist with asset-protection planning during life and with wealth-transfer planning at death. On the other hand, use of a business entity may complicate funding of a private foundation with artwork and/or copyrights during life or at death.
- Specifics with respect to copyright laws. Remember that the artist generally retains the copyright to self-created works after sale of the work itself.
- Terms of any contracts of sale that the artist may enter into with buyers or with galleries who represent artists.

Gifting During Life

The discussion of gifting during life, in chapter 10, is the starting point for gifts made during life by artists. However, the nature of self-created art makes giving during life more challenging for artists.

It is important to remember that in the case of a gift, the general rule is that the donee of the gift will receive the gift with the donor's basis. In the case of a collector, it is fairly easy to determine what that basis is; it will generally be the purchase price paid for the artwork, plus any improvements such as restoration or framing.

The same may not hold true for a gift from an artist. The artist's cost basis is the amount paid for supplies to create the work of art. The amount of the gift, for calculating federal gift tax consequences, is its fair market value at the time of the gift (which must be determined by appraisal if over $15,000), but the cost basis is the assumed much lesser amount of the cost of supplies—perhaps a few hundred dollars, if that.

As a result, the benefit of gifting (removing future appreciation above the fair market value at the time of the gift from the artist's estate—the same as with a collector, as discussed in chapter 10) may be less for an artist than for a collector. This is not due to technical reasons but simply due to the fact that the carryover cost basis will be much lower. As a result, the donee recipient of the gift will incur taxes on a greater amount if they subsequently sell the piece.

An even more significant impediment to gifting by an artist is that the art is ordinary income property in the hands of the artist, meaning that if it is sold by the artist, any gain above the cost of producing the art is ordinary income.

The art retains that character if gifted during life. Therefore, if the donee subsequently sells the art, any gain will be taxable as ordinary income. If the donee subsequently decides to donate the art to charity, the donee will be limited to the artist's cost basis when determining their federal income tax charitable deduction because the art retains its character as ordinary income property.

In summary, gifting during life may lead to significant wealth transfer, just as with collectors. However, because of a presumed much lower carryover basis and the retained character of the art in the donee's hands, the net benefit to the artist's family or friends may not be as great as to the donees of collectors.

Donating During Life

As discussed in chapter 11, art is a capital asset in the hands of an art collector or investor. This is not true for an artist, and self-created art is ordinary income property for purposes of determining the federal income tax charitable deduction. You may recall that this is the least favorable category of property to donate, as it will always result in a federal income tax charitable deduction equal to the lesser of fair market value or cost basis, almost always the latter. Furthermore, the artist would need to donate both the art and the copyright to qualify for a federal income tax charitable deduction because of the partial interest rule discussed in chapter 11. As a result, it is unlikely that an artist will make significant donations of self-created art during life.

An artist may still wish to donate art to one or more museums, as having their art accepted and displayed by a museum enhances the value of their art overall. In such a case, it may be preferable to donate the art, retain the copyright for future planning, and forgo any federal income tax charitable deduction, as it will be relatively small in any case.

Charitable remainder trusts (CRTs), discussed in chapter 11, are rarely used by collectors. Although it is technically possible for an artist to use a CRT to defer ordinary income from an occasional sale of art, it is perhaps even rarer to encounter this planning tool used for artists than for collectors. Again, using a CRT during life would require that both the art and the copyright be contributed to the CRT.

As discussed below, a number of commercially successful artists have and are creating "artist-funded foundations." Although it is common to create the foundation during life, it is rare that any significant funding will occur during life, especially with artwork, because the federal income tax charitable deduction would be limited to cost basis. Furthermore, it is often desirable to separate the copyright from the art for planning purposes, which would eliminate any federal income tax charitable deduction.

Summary

The character of self-created art makes it difficult to conduct tax-efficient planning during life. A sale will be taxed as ordinary income, a gift will result in both carryover basis and carryover character of property, and a charitable donation will result in virtually no federal income tax charitable deduction. Therefore, it is more likely that any planning done during the life of the artist will take effect at death.

This does not mean that the successful artist should forgo planning. Certainly, they should complete basic estate planning, including a will and ancillary documents such as powers of attorney for business and health-care matters. And a structure can be put into place to be funded and implemented at death. However, significant tax and financial planning is better left to take effect at death rather than during life.

18

Testamentary Planning

From both a tax and a nontax point of view, the importance of planning for the artist's estate has taken on more significance with the growing number of commercially successful artists.[1]

Galleries, auction houses, and certain financial services firms have all recognized this and have increased their focus and capacity to work specifically with artists' estates. Because of the nature of self-created assets, most planning for artists that is undertaken during life will not take effect until death.

Selling at Death

At the artist's death, the basis of their self-created art is stepped up to fair market value, which is the value that will also be used for estate tax calculation purposes. As a result, pre-death appreciation will avoid federal income tax. Equally important, the character of the art changes from ordinary income property to capital property, so that post-death, presale appreciation is taxed at lower capital gain rates, assuming that the estate is not deemed to be conducting an active trade or business but is merely engaged in the orderly disposition of an estate. This is essentially the same federal income tax treatment as for a collector or investor.

Expenses of selling the art, including gallery or dealer commissions, should be deductible as estate administration expenses. This again is similar to the treatment that would be received by the estate of a collector or an investor.

The biggest challenges for an artist's estate are valuation (see the discussion of the blockage discount below) and the orderly disposition of what is likely to be a significant amount of artwork. Both of these issues are further discussed below.

Gifting (Bequeathing) at Death

As discussed in chapter 17, gifting during life is often disadvantageous for the artist and their family. The constraints of carryover basis and carryover of the character of property as ordinary income property go away at death. At that point, the basis in the property "steps up" to its fair market value, and the character of the art changes to a capital asset in the hands of an individual who inherits from the artist. As such, with several exceptions discussed below, all of the discussion in chapter 13 relating to noncharitable transfers at death applies to the artist's estate.

All of the art, as well as other assets, is part of the estate and will be subject to the same federal estate tax rules discussed in chapter 13.

Blockage Discount

A significant issue faced by an artist's estate that is not normally faced by a collector's estate is valuation—and, more specifically, whether a "blockage discount" applies and, if so, how much. This is significant both for calculating the value of the estate for purposes of paying estate taxes and for valuing charitable transfers taking place at death.

According to Treasury regulations and case law, when determining the estate tax liability of an artist's estate, the estate must not only value the individual pieces of art but also consider whether the aggregate value of the art should be reduced for a blockage discount. This is a downward adjustment made to reflect the economic reality that introducing a large supply of art by the same artist into the market will decrease the price of individual works. To determine the appropriate value of the estate for the purposes of estate tax liability, appraisers apply a blockage discount to reflect the realities of the marketplace economics.

The concept of blockage discounts is rooted in the basic standard for determining the value of any estate, "fair market value." According to Treasury Regulation § 20.2031-1, the fair market value of property is the price at which the property would change hands between a willing buyer and a willing seller. "Willing" means that neither the buyer nor the seller is compelled to buy or sell, forcing the price to be artificially high or low. Under the regulations, it is assumed that both parties have reasonable knowledge of the relevant facts and that the market in which the sale would occur is the market in which the item at issue is most commonly sold to the public. When determining the value of a large collection of art belonging to a single artist, the estate must consider the potential buyer and market for the collection as a whole, as well as for the individual pieces of art.

To determine when to apply a blockage discount, appraisers and executors rely on the Treasury regulation for valuing a large number of shares of stock. That regulation permits a blockage discount if the executor can show that the block of stock to be valued is so large in relation to the actual sales on the existing market that it could not be liquidated in a reasonable time without depressing the market. More simply, the concept of supply and demand underlies this rule.

The courts have applied the securities valuation regulation to determine the value of a large block of art held by an estate. The U.S. Tax Court first applied the concept of blockage discounts to art in 1972 in the case *Estate of David Smith v. Commissioner*. David Smith owned 425 pieces of his sculpture at the time of his death. The executors of his estate first estimated its value by calculating the individual price of each work at the time of Smith's death and totaling these values for a sum of $4,284,000. The estate then applied a blockage discount of 75 percent, claiming that at the time of death the works could be sold only to a bulk purchaser acquiring the art for resale. Such a purchaser would pay only 25 percent of the art's aggregate value, with the understanding that an acceptable profit could be recovered only over an extended period of time.

The IRS rejected the estate's blockage discount and valued the works at $4,284,000, their full fair market value. According to the IRS, selling all of the sculptures simultaneously would not have an adverse impact on the fair market value of each item. The Smith estate then petitioned the Tax Court for further review.

The Tax Court agreed with the Smith estate that the blockage discount should apply to collections of art. The court explained that the IRS should have considered that a willing buyer of one piece of art would take into account that 424 other similar items were being offered for sale at the same time and would lower their price accordingly. The court emphasized that a large number of similar works would significantly impact the auction market, the typical market for this type of property, and that any valuation analysis should account for this material factor. In applying the blockage discount, the court also considered Smith's reputation, the size and quality of the 425 sculptures, and the location of the bulk of these sculptures, among other factors.

While the Tax Court agreed with the Smith estate about the application of the blockage discount, it ultimately concluded that a 75 percent discount was too much and held that the fair market value of the 425 sculptures at the moment of Smith's death was $2,700,000, representing a discount of 37 percent. The court did not provide any specific analysis about how it reached this figure.

About 20 years later, the Tax Court considered another blockage discount for the estate of Georgia O'Keeffe. At the time of her death, O'Keeffe's estate comprised approximately 400 works that she had created. In her will, O'Keeffe had bequeathed 42 works to eight museums. The total value of the bequeathed works was $22,575,000. As calculated by the estate, the sum of the individual fair market values of O'Keeffe's works on the date of her death exceeded $72,000,000.

When determining the tax liability of the estate, experts for the estate applied a 75 percent blockage discount. Similar to the Smith estate, the O'Keeffe estate assumed that all of the works could be hypothetically sold only to a single buyer as a bulk purchase. The IRS did not follow this analysis but divided the works in the estate into two categories: bequeathed art and remaining art. The bequeathed works were not available for sale, according to the IRS, and thus did not require a blockage discount. The IRS, apparently following *Smith*, then applied a discount of 37 percent to the remaining art, finding that the estate owed $6,014,493 in taxes. The estate petitioned the Tax Court for review of this deficiency.

The Tax Court in *Estate of Georgia O'Keeffe* disagreed with both the estate and the IRS. First, the Tax Court objected to the IRS not applying the discount to the bequeathed art, as the fair market value analysis assumes that all works held by the estate are available for sale, regardless of the final disposition of the property. However, the court also rejected the estate's assumptions that there must be only a single buyer and that the property must change hands at the date of death because this approach ignores the regulatory condition that the willing buyer and willing seller would act without compulsion.

The Tax Court ultimately held that a blockage discount should apply. Acknowledging that different works within the estate would be of interest to different segments of the market, the court determined that there would not be one buyer, like the estate's proposed single bulk purchaser, but several buyers, with multiple sales transpiring over a period of time. The court proposed that O'Keeffe's work should be divided into two categories for these potential sales: works that could be sold within a relatively short time period at approximately their individual values and works that could be marketed only over a long period of years with substantial effort. The quality, uniqueness, and salability of each respective work would determine placement in a particular category. The court further proposed that the latter group should be discounted at 75 percent and the former group should be discounted at 25 percent. According to the court, the fair market value of the entire estate, with the discount, was $36,400,000, leaving the IRS to determine the final tax liability for the estate.

Unlike the *Smith* and *O'Keeffe* cases, the case of *Calder v. Commissioner* addressed the blockage discount issue in the context of gift taxes. Alexander Calder died in 1976, and his widow, Louisa Calder, inherited 1,226 gouaches. The 1,226 gouaches were listed as part of a collection of 1,292 gouaches on the estate tax return filed by the Calder estate. The total fair market value of the 1,292 gouaches listed on the tax return was $949,750 after a blockage discount of 60 percent. The IRS did not dispute this value at the time the estate tax return was filed.

After Alexander Calder's death, Louisa Calder created four irrevocable trusts for her children and grandchildren. She then gifted the gouaches to the trusts: 306 gouaches to each of the trusts of her two daughters and 307 gouaches to each of the trusts of the grandchildren. Subsequently, 369 of the gouaches were sold by the trusts between 1977 and 1984.

On her 1976 gift tax return, Louisa Calder estimated that the fair market value of the gouaches did not vary between the date of Alexander Calder's death and the date of the gift and applied the same 60 percent blockage discount, reporting a value of $949,750. The IRS calculated the value of the gifts to be $2,300,000, rejecting the use of the blockage discount for the gift tax. According to the IRS, blockage discounts were inappropriate in this context because gifts, unlike deaths, are contemplated events and can accommodate the market accordingly.

While all parties stipulated to the fair market value of the individual gouaches, the legal issue before the Tax Court was whether a blockage discount should be applied when valuing gifts and, if so, whether the discount should be applied to each gift separately or on an aggregate basis. The court ultimately held that blockage discounts may apply to gifts and that the blockage discount should be applied separately to each gift, citing the Treasury regulations that outline the same treatment for the valuation of a block of stocks distributed as multiple, separate gifts.

To determine the precise discount, the Tax court used the same approach for valuing annuities by considering the rate of liquidation at a uniform rate over a period of time. Relying on the actual average sales figures of the gouaches already sold during the 1977–1984 period, the court found that 60 gouaches could be sold each year and that it would take 22 years to liquidate all 1,226 gouaches. Using an annuity framework, the court applied a 10 percent discount rate over the 22-year liquidation period to the per-item fair market value of the gouaches, resulting in a total valuation of $1,210,000. The court left the determination of the final tax liability calculation to the IRS.

As challenging as it is to determine the fair market value of an individual painting, calculating the value of a collection of hundreds of similar pieces is that much more difficult. Although the Treasury regulations do not specifically provide for a blockage discount for art and other collectibles, the Tax Court has applied a blockage discount to estates and gifts of artists. These cases reveal multiple factors to consider when calculating a blockage discount, including the potential buyer, the salability of the type of works, the artist's reputation, and the potential rate of sale. The ongoing case involving the de Kooning estate presents slightly different facts, as it is not the estate of the artist but that of the artist's daughter. However, hopefully the Tax Court will provide further guidance as to the application of blockage discounts to art held by an estate.[2]

Donating at Death

As mentioned above, if the artist owns a collection of work by other artists, then the considerations for donating at death are the same as for the collector, as discussed in chapter 14.

To the extent that the artist wishes to make bequests of self-created artwork, the federal estate tax charitable deduction will be equal to the fair market value of the artwork, not the cost basis (which would typically be used to calculate the federal income tax charitable deduction for donations during life). This is true whether the donation is to a public charity or to the artist's own foundation. This is subject to several important considerations.

First, artwork being left to charity should be specifically identified. This is true for noncharitable bequests of artwork as well.

Second, any blockage discount, as discussed above, must be taken into account. For charitable donations, this should have a net zero effect—both the value of the estate and the value of the contribution should be reduced by the same amount of blockage discount.

Third, it is possible—in fact common—to split the copyright from the piece of artwork itself. In this case, one—the art or the copyright—may be donated to charity (including the artist's own foundation) and the other bequeathed to the family. This allows the retention of some value by the family, as well as the contribution of art to charity. However, this type of planning must be done carefully.

Normally, donations at death do not involve the related-use rule, discussed in chapter 11. That rule is primarily a federal income tax rule pertaining to the calculation of the amount of the charitable deduction. However, a charitable bequest by an artist may involve a separate related-use rule found in IRC § 2055(e)(4)(C). That section denies an estate tax charitable deduction for certain split-interest transfers, which may inadvertently happen because the artwork and the copyright are viewed as separate property interests at death (though not during life). What is permissible is the transfer of the artwork to a qualified charity, which includes a POF but not a private grant-making foundation, and the retention of the copyright by the estate.

Other Artist Issues at Death

Any planning for an artist should include appropriate planning around copyrights. It is advisable to include an intellectual property expert on the planning team to ensure that any intellectual property is properly incorporated into the overall estate and financial plan. A full discussion of copyright rules is beyond the scope of this book—and beyond the scope of the author's knowledge.

In addition to the valuation considerations discussed above, the artist will likely own a significant amount of self-created artwork at death, and its ultimate disposal will need to be addressed. This is one of the primary motivations for creating an artist-funded foundation, discussed below. Absent such a foundation, there should be a plan in place for a gallery, or other agent, to manage the sale of inventory over a period of time to maximize the value of the artwork.

Summary

Most planning for artists will take effect at death, whether it involves sale, bequest, or charitable donation. The fact that there will be significant inventory in the estate affects valuation and necessitates continuing representation to oversee an orderly liquidation of self-created works.

Notes

1. *See, e.g.*, Sarah P. Hanson, *The Great Artists' Estates Race*, Art Newsl., May 17, 2017.

2. For blockage discounts, *see* Ralph E. Lerner & Judith Bresler, Art Law 1410–1422 (Practising Law Inst., 4th ed. 2012); Ronald D. Spencer, *Blockage Discounts Valuing Art Collections*, 6 Spencer's Art L.J., no. 1 (Winter 2015/2016).

19

Artist-Funded Foundations

An increasingly common planning technique for commercially successful artists is known as an "artist-funded foundation." An artist-funded foundation can

- Serve as a repository for the artist's works;
- Raise and maintain awareness of the artist;
- Maintain and preserve the artist's legacy;
- Facilitate the orderly disposition of the artist's inventory of works;
- Facilitate scholarly research and study and, in certain instances, serve as the ultimate authority as to authenticity of an artist's works; and
- Support other philanthropic goals of the artist, which may or may not be otherwise related to the artist's works.

Although an artist-funded foundation may be formed at death, it is often preferable to form the foundation during the life of the artist and to fund it with some level of cash or assets other than self-created works (which would entitle the artist only to a cost-basis deduction for federal income tax purposes).

The primary funding of the foundation will likely occur at the death of the artist, and the estate will generally be entitled to a full fair market value estate tax charitable deduction, subject to any blockage discount. The funding may include some or all of the artist's remaining self-created works, copyrights, archival materials, and additional cash or other property. In some instances, the foundation may own and maintain the artist's home and studio.

The foundation, whether formed during life or at the death of the artist, will be subject to the private foundation rules. The private foundation rules are a series of excise taxes imposed to deter certain behaviors by private foundations and their "disqualified persons."

POF or Not?

Which of these private foundation rules apply will depend in part on whether the artist-funded foundation is a private operating foundation (POF) or a private nonoperating foundation. The latter does not conduct charitable activities itself but rather makes grants to other operating charities.

A nonoperating, or grant-making, foundation is the default choice; that is, all charitable organizations are private nonoperating foundations unless they can establish that they qualify for the preferential POF treatment. However, that is not a "check the box" decision; rather, it depends on the activities of the foundation. There are specific tests, outlined in "Your Own Museum" in chapter 11, that must be passed to be a POF.

The decision as to whether or not the artist-funded foundation should be a POF is significant. If the artist wishes to bequeath works of art to the foundation but the copyrights to such works to another, noncharitable beneficiary, then the artworks will need to be bequeathed to a POF, not a grant-making foundation, for the estate to be entitled to an estate tax charitable deduction.[1]

Foundation Excise Taxes

For all private foundations, there are six excise taxes that apply to funding and operations. These excise taxes set the boundaries for an artist-funded foundation's activities. Substantial penalties apply for violating any of the excise taxes, regardless of intent. The artist, if the foundation is formed during life, or the artist's estate, if the foundation is formed at death, will be a substantial contributor and, hence, a disqualified person. Disqualified persons also include (1) the artist's family members and related entities, (2) foundation managers and their family members and related entities, and (3) substantial contributors to the foundation and their family members and related entities.

A full discussion of all of the rules and regulations applicable to private foundations is beyond the scope of this book. For those who wish to delve further into this topic, a comprehensive resource is BNA Portfolio # 815. Following is a brief description of the excise taxes and their applicability to artist-funded foundations.

All private foundations are subject to a 2 percent excise tax on their net investment income, which may be reduced to 1 percent in certain instances. This excise tax cannot be avoided, but it is only 2 percent (or 1 percent) of net income, not assets. It does mean that the foundation will pay a 2 percent (or 1 percent) tax on any gain on the sale of any art even if the art was held as a charitable-use asset.[2]

Probably the most significant potential excise tax exposure is for a violation of the self-dealing rules found in IRC § 4941. These rules limit transactions between the foundation and its disqualified persons. Unless a specific exception applies, no financial transactions—direct or indirect— are allowed between the foundation and its disqualified persons. Furthermore, these rules preclude an artist-funded foundation from engaging in any programs or activities (including grant making) that promote an artist's work during the artist's lifetime. This is another reason for the artist to wait until death to make a significant contribution of self-created work to their foundation.

There are a number of rulings involving self-dealing and art owned by private foundations. Some of these transactions are rather obvious, others are not:

- Display of Art
  - ~ In Revenue Ruling 74-600, 1974-2 C.B. 835, the IRS ruled that the display of three paintings owned by a private foundation in the residence of a disqualified person constituted self-dealing even

though the home was open to the public several times each year and approximately 2,000 people visited to view the paintings as well as the private collection.

~ In Private Letter Ruling 94-08-006 (Feb. 25, 1994), the IRS revoked a foundation's exemption after finding that the primary activity of the foundation was to display and otherwise promote an artist who was a disqualified person.

- Purchase or Sale of Art
  ~ In Revenue Ruling 76-18, 1976-1 C.B. 355, the IRS ruled that a foundation's sale of art at a public auction to a disqualified person was self-dealing.
  ~ Private Letter Ruling 78-24-001 (Dec. 12, 1977) found that a foundation's purchase of art from a disqualified person was an act of self-dealing.
  ~ Private Letter Ruling 83-10-002 (1983) ruled that a museum's use of grant money to purchase art from disqualified persons was self-dealing.

- Loan of Art
  ~ In Private Letter Ruling 91-39-024 (July 1, 1991), the IRS ruled that the loan of artwork by a disqualified person to a foundation without charge was not self-dealing. Furthermore, in Private Letter Rulings 91-39-024, 88-42-045, and 2014-23-033, under various facts, the IRS ruled that a foundation's payment of expenses for storing, transporting, conserving, and insuring works of art that were loaned to the foundation for display would not be self-dealing because any benefit to the disqualified person would be merely incidental.

- Payment of Compensation
  ~ An exception to the self-dealing prohibition exists for the payment of reasonable compensation for specified personal services. In Private Letter Ruling 90-11-050, this was found to include the payment of commissions to disqualified persons for the sale of art owned by a foundation. However, such was not the case in *Estate of Reis v. Commissioner*, 87 T.C. 1016 (1986), where a 50 percent commission paid by the estate to a disqualified person with respect to a beneficiary of the estate was found by the Tax Court to be indirect self-dealing.

The point of these rulings and cases is that one must be careful when conducting business with a foundation to ensure that no direct or indirect self-dealing takes place. Again, intent is irrelevant for these purposes.

Private grant-making foundations, but not POFs, must distribute their income in furtherance of charitable activities. This rule is often expressed as requiring the foundation to distribute 5 percent of its noncharitable-use, or investment, assets each year. It is rare that foundations run afoul of this rule, as the exact amount must be calculated and reported on the foundation's tax return, Form 990-PF, which must be filed each year.

The bigger issue is not the 5 percent calculation but which assets must be included when determining the base on which the 5 percent is calculated. For an artist-funded foundation, or any private foundation that owns artwork, a determination must be made as to whether the artwork is a charitable-use asset; that is, is it being used to further the foundation's charitable purpose? That in turn depends on whether the art is being actively marketed for sale (an investment asset that must be counted) or held for charitable use, such as being loaned out for exhibit, scholarly research or study, or other similar activities. A Revenue Ruling and several Private Letter Rulings have held that artworks owned by a foundation and used in active public exhibition programs were considered to be charitable-use assets and not subject to the 5 percent payout calculation.[3]

This issue is more complicated if the art is loaned to a foreign charity. Gifts of art or cash to foreign charities will count toward the 5 percent, as long as "expenditure responsibility" is conducted or an "equivalency determination" is made with respect to any such foreign gifts. The latter is preferable, as the former will require a continuous process for as long as the art is on loan.

Private foundations are restricted in the amount of controlling business interests they may own: generally 20 percent of voting control (including the interests owned by disqualified persons). It is unlikely that an artist-funded foundation will encounter this problem unless the artist operates their business in a corporate or partnership form and then bequeaths that ownership to the foundation. In such a case, the foundation could continue to own the business interest if it maintains ownership only for up to five years, with a possible extension of an additional five years, or if the business is functionally related to the activities of the foundation.

There are several Private Letter Rulings that discuss functionally related businesses involving artists. The one most closely related to visual artists is Private Letter Ruling 2013-23-029 (Mar. 12, 2013), which ruled that a foundation's receipt of stock of a corporation that owned art and copyrights of an artist constituted a functionally related business. The corporation employed individuals who had worked with the artist while alive and who had managed the artist's business. As a result, the IRS felt that the corporation and the foundation had the same mission of promoting the legacy and the works of the artist.[4]

Private foundations, including artist-funded foundations, are prohibited from making investments that jeopardize their tax-exempt purpose. This excise tax applies only to investments made by the foundation, not to investments given or bequeathed to the foundation. In addition, program-related investments (PRIs), which are investments made primarily to accomplish a tax-exempt purpose rather than as a normal investment, are not considered jeopardy investments. Therefore, it is unlikely that a properly managed artist-funded foundation will incur this tax.

Foundations are not permitted to make "taxable expenditures" under IRC § 4945. Taxable expenditures include payments made to support lobbying or other attempts to influence legislation or elections. Taxable expenditures also include grants made to individuals under certain circumstances unless preapproved by the IRS. Finally, taxable expenditures include grants to certain other charities, or to foreign charities, absent conducting expenditure responsibility (a sort of due diligence to ensure that gifts are used for charitable purposes) or obtaining an equivalency determination (in effect, a statement that the charity would be qualified under U.S. law). The latter is preferable, as the exercise of expenditure responsibility over a gift of artwork may require expenditure responsibility reporting in perpetuity.

Just as with any private foundation, appropriate governance measures should be undertaken. This includes the adoption of an appropriate mission statement—supporting the artist's legacy, plus any other charitable mission that the artist wishes to support—which drives the spending policy, which in turn drives the investment policy covering both the art and other financial assets. Governance also includes selecting an appropriate board of trustees or directors and adopting appropriate policy statements.[5]

Unrelated Business Taxable Income

Artist-funded foundations, like all private foundations, are exempt from federal income tax (other than the excise tax on net investment income discussed above). However, as with all tax-exempt entities, an artist-funded foundation is subject to the unrelated business income tax (UBIT) on its unrelated business income (UBI). This includes any net income that it receives from a trade or business activity that is not related to the tax-exempt purpose of the foundation and any debt-financed investment income. Furthermore, if the artist-funded foundation engages in more than an insubstantial amount of activities unrelated to its tax-exempt purpose, it may actually lose its tax exemption.

The activity that poses the greatest danger for an artist-funded foundation is the sale of works of art in the same manner as a commercial gallery. Conversely, if the foundation owns the copyrights, it may license such copyrights or other intellectual property and receive royalties, which are not considered to be UBI, as long as no services are provided in connection with such licensing.[6]

Summary

For both tax and nontax reasons, the use of an artist-funded foundation makes a great deal of sense for the commercially successful artist. It is an estate tax efficient planning technique that also allows for the preservation of the artist's legacy, and allows for effective control over the remaining inventory of the artist.

Notes

1. IRC § 2055(e)(4).
2. Rev. Rul. 74-498, 1974-2 C.B. 387; I.R.S. Priv. Ltr. Rul. 2007-34-024 (May 30, 2007); I.R.S. Priv. Ltr. Rul. 83-52-098 (Sept. 30, 1983); I.R.S. Priv. Ltr. Rul. 78-42-044 (July 19, 1978); I.R.S. Priv. Ltr. Rul. 94-11-009 (Dec. 10, 1993).

3. IRC § 4940.

4. *See also* I.R.S. Priv. Ltr. Ruls. 89-30-047 (May 2, 1989) and 85-41-107 (July 19, 1985), which also discuss what constitutes a functionally related business.

5. BNA portfolio no. 815.

6. IRC § 512(b)(2).

Resources

Following are selected resources that the reader may wish to consult for additional information.

General Reference Books

Lerner, Ralph E., and Judith Bresler. *Art Law.* 4th ed. New York: Practising Law Institute, 2012. The most comprehensive work on all aspects of art law.

Mendelsohn, Michael. *Life Is Short, Art Is Long.* 2nd ed. New York: Acanthus Press, 2006–2007. A comprehensive treatment of the topic, similar in scope to this book.

Rozell, Mary. *The Art Collector's Handbook: A Guide to Collection Management and Care.* London: Lund Humphries, 2014. Discusses the practical and financial implications of owning and maintaining art.

Woodham, Doug. *Art Collecting Today: Market Insights for Everyone Passionate About Art.* New York: Allworth Press, 2017. Crucial reading for anyone collecting art today.

General Reference Articles

Horwood, Richard M. "Life Is Short, Art Endures: Issues for Collectors and Their Heirs." *Family Foundation Advisor* 11, no. 1 (November/December 2011).

Leibell, David T., and Daniel L. Daniels. "Practical Planning Strategies for Art and Collectibles." Thomson Reuters/RIA (2010).

Interesting Reading/Just Plain Fun

I typed "stolen art" into the search engine for "books" on Amazon.com, and the result was 1,198 selections! I obviously did not read all of those, but a few of my favorites are listed below.

Edsel, Robert M. *The Monuments Men: Allied Heroes, Nazi Thieves, and the Greatest Treasure Hunt in History.* New York: Center Street, 2009.

Findlay, Michael. *The Value of Art: Money, Power, Beauty.* Munich: Prestel, 2012. An interesting examination of the world of modern art, written by an insider.

Honan, William H. *Treasure Hunt: A New York Times Reporter Tracks the Quedlinburg Hoard.* New York: Fromm International, 1997.

Nicholas, Lynn H. *The Rape of Europa: The Fate of Europe's Treasures in the Third Reich and the Second World War.* New York: Vintage, 1995.

O'Connor, Mary. *The Lady in Gold: The Extraordinary Tale of Gustav Klimt's Masterpiece, Portrait of Adele Bloch-Bauer.* New York: Vintage, 2015.

Wittman, Robert K. *Priceless.* New York: Broadway Books, 2010. Written by the founder of the FBI Art Crime Team.

And for the movie buffs out there:

The Art of the Steal, directed by Don Argott (IFC Films, 2009). A documentary about the Barnes Collection in Philadelphia. Although biased, it is an interesting examination of donor intent and how changed circumstances can lead to an outcome totally different from what was contemplated by the donor. Currently available on Netflix.

Stolen, directed by Rebecca Dreyfus (Persistence of Vision Films, 2006). A movie about the Gardner theft and attempts to solve the heist and recover the art. *The Thomas Crown Affair,* directed by John McTiernan (United Artists/Metro-Goldwyn-Mayer, 1999). Pierce Brosnan and Rene Russo star in this 1999 remake of the 1968 original. Currently available on Netflix.

Index